Tom Boyd was an outstanding youth athlete, destined from childhood for a career in professional sports. At the age of eighteen, he joined the GWS Giants as the AFL's number 1 draft pick and was later recruited to play for the Western Bulldogs on a record $7 million contract. In 2016 Tom was instrumental in the Bulldog's drought-breaking Premiership win, playing arguably the greatest game of his career and helping steer the team to ultimate victory. However, in 2019, following years of struggle with depression and anxiety, Tom made the decision to walk away from the AFL, leaving the fame and success of football behind him for a happier life. Tom is now a public speaker and mental health advocate. *Nowhere to Hide* is his first book.

For Anna and Armani
I hope I make you proud

TOM BOYD
NOWHERE
TO HIDE

A memoir of football, mental health and resilience

ALLEN&UNWIN
SYDNEY • MELBOURNE • AUCKLAND • LONDON

First published in 2022

Allen & Unwin
83 Alexander Street
Crows Nest NSW 2065
Cammeraygal
Australia
Phone: (61 2) 8425 0100
Email: info@allenandunwin.com
Web: www.allenandunwin.com

Allen & Unwin acknowledges the traditional owners of the lands on which we
live and work. We pay our respects to all Aboriginal and Torres Strait Islander
elders, past and present.

A catalogue record for this
book is available from the
National Library of Australia

ISBN 978 1 76106 549 1

Set in 12.75/18.5 pt Adobe Garamond Pro by Midland Typesetters, Australia

CONTENTS

Prologue   1

1   Measuring Up   5

2   Commitment   13

3   Recognition   25

4   Dress Rehearsal   53

5   Bittersweet   87

6   Trapped   121

7   Desperation   143

8   Scrutiny   175

9   Connection   211

10 Stress Test   255

11 Time and Space   293

Epilogue   323

PROLOGUE

1 OCTOBER 2016

Sitting on the field of the MCG, having just won an AFL Premiership, I felt like a titan. I had played out the moments of that day countless times in my mind, not just in the lead-up to the game but all my life. I had dreamed of winning a Premiership, of being the hero, kicking the big goal and taking the big mark. And everything I had ever dreamed of had just come true.

Sitting next to me was Joel Hamling, another Bulldog hero. We laughed and smiled as we soaked in every ounce of joy that surrounded us, from the field up to the furthest reaches of the great coliseum that is the Melbourne Cricket Ground. It was magical. Red, white and blue confetti rained down on us, painting the once-green playing field of the MCG in the Bulldogs' colours. Tens of thousands of people cheered, singing the club's theme song as it played, over and over again. Fans of all ages hugged each other. Some cried, others laughed, some hollered with so much bravado that it almost seemed like they had been on the field, playing alongside us. Every single Bulldogs fan in the stadium, from the lifelong supporters to allies who had donned a Footscray scarf for the day, cheered the first Premiership the club had won in 62 years.

I could barely comprehend it. This was the biggest moment of my life and I knew that it would be an incredible moment in my football career, but it was impossible for me, at 21, to truly understand what this meant for the people around me. I couldn't really grasp what it meant for those who had played their entire career at the club, men like Matthew Boyd and Dale Morris, or for those who had become Bulldogs in their fathers' footsteps, like Tom Liberatore, Lachie Hunter and Liam Picken.

I loved all of my teammates in that moment, but I was most comfortable next to Joel. We were both at our second AFL club, having arrived together two years earlier. I didn't share that overwhelming sense felt by many of release, 62 years in the making, but the intensity of the moment still swallowed me up. I had played the game of a lifetime, been one of the best players on the ground, and had just kicked a goal which I knew would go down in history. That was enough.

Soon, Joel and I were joined by the man who was perhaps

the single most instrumental figure in the Bulldogs' success, club president Peter Gordon. He and I grasped the cup together, Peter doing his best impression of an actual bulldog, and the moment was snapped into eternity by the swarms of photographers.

It was a special moment for us. We said little, but felt a lot. Peter had given everything for his club, over decades, to rescue the team from bankruptcy and create for us the chance to experience the ultimate victory. I knew he had taken a risk on me, offering a seven-year deal to a green eighteen-year-old hopeful. He was given no shortage of criticism for that choice but he had weathered the storm, resolutely supporting me, and I had finally repaid his faith in me.

Peter was one of the few people who had a true sense of what I had been through in my career, but even he was broadly unaware of the mental health struggles I had been wrestling with for years. Though I had dreamed about this day since I was a boy, it had felt like it would never happen, that I wouldn't be playing football long enough to enjoy this moment of success.

Every step along the way, ever since I was drafted, had felt like an uphill battle: I had to perform and win for my own self-esteem. Over the years, severe anxiety had led to sleepless nights, and sleepless nights had led to deep feelings of sadness and hopelessness. More times than I could count, I had questioned why I was playing professional football at all.

I had struggled privately, joylessly, for so long. This was my long road to an AFL Premiership. This was the story that did not make the headlines.

Holding that cup, I tried to make sense of the moment. My senses had been dialled up to eleven while I gave all my attention to the task of winning a football game. Now, with that military focus gone, the commotion around me was giving me a sensory overload, as if I were staring into the sun. *What am I feeling?* Was it vindication, after all the criticism that had been hurled at me? *No, it couldn't be.* Was it satisfaction? *Not really.* It felt more like relief. I was relieved. *It's all been worth it.*

I'm a Premiership player, I thought. *They can never take this away from me. Everything is going to be different now.*

In a way, I was right. My name would be enshrined in gold in the Western Bulldogs' locker room, forever. I would be reminded of that day for years to come. I would always be Tom Boyd, Premiership Player. But all the glory couldn't change who I was, deep down—an insecure 21-year-old who was in an ongoing battle with depression and anxiety. I thought that moment would wipe away every doubt, every sadness, every fear inside me, but the road ahead was never going to be that easy.

1

MEASURING UP

As early as I can remember, my time was spent around football clubs. Players, coaches, officials and volunteers were the people who shaped much of my young life. From the age of three, I was running around on the cold, muddy ground at Mullum Mullum Reserve in Ringwood, the home ground of my local club, Norwood, just like my dad, Geoff, had done before me. In the old, nicotine-stained clubrooms there was an iconic photo of Dad hoisting the 1989 Eastern District League Premiership cup as captain-coach, surrounded by teammates and covered in beer. It was a real family affair.

Not long after I began playing at the club, I became a waterboy for the senior team. At first, I was terrified of the bodies flying past me, the off chance the ball might come near me. But I was most intimidated by the senior players, who would scream at me for a drink: 'Give us a squirt, NOW!' I quickly learned to avoid the worst of them, picking a different end of the ground to run water and looking after some of my idols, including Scott 'Daigo' Day and a long, spindly ruckman who was nicknamed 'Monkey' because of his comically long arms. I'd usually have a basketball game to play in the morning, so after running water for the senior match I'd be exhausted. Still, I always felt sheepish walking into the club treasurer's office to ask for the $10 I'd earned.

Dad coached me through my first two years of football, in the under-8s and under-9s. I loved everything about it. I loved the dew and frost on the ground on a winter morning, shivering in my boots alongside my footy mates. The training sessions were fun back then, filled with games, drills and mud. The only thing Dad insisted on was that we learned to kick the ball well. Even when I was small, Dad pushed me to develop the skill. It was something he had always prided himself on as a player—he'd famously come in just behind Wayne Harmes in a long-kicking competition one time—and he was adamant I would be a good kick as well.

The two of us would sneak in some extra skills practice during the week—and if I missed a kick, Dad was unforgiving. 'Go and get it yourself,' he would say, or 'What's that rubbish?' I went through a stage where I was trying to kick around corners all the time, doing strange and funky kicking motions for no apparent reason, and Dad very sternly told me that if I wasn't going to kick the ball properly, we were going to go home. He was firm with me, but he wasn't a bully. He was just a no-nonsense kind of guy.

Dad also taught me how to wash and shine my boots, making sure the Dubbin was heavily applied. We made countless attempts to make a store-bought mouthguard mould properly to my teeth. They were ghastly things to wear, but as Dad always said, matter-of-factly, 'If you break your teeth, they don't grow back.'

I was grateful for the extra time we spent together because of football. When he wasn't at the club, Dad was moving through the ranks of the commercial electrical outfit that he would later own, while simultaneously scrounging out as many domestic jobs as he could to make ends meet. I rarely saw him during the week, as he would be gone before I woke up in the morning and often came home after I went to bed.

Dad had left school at the start of Form IV, the equivalent of Year Ten in those days. He was called into the vice-principal's office for some indiscretion and given a little push: 'Geoff, I'm not sure this school thing is for you—why don't you get a job?' That's exactly what Dad did. He started his electrical apprenticeship shortly afterwards, the career he would be in until the day he retired, and he never looked back. Before long, Dad's leadership and work ethic began to shine through. He worked days, nights, interstate and weekends if he could, never missing an opportunity to get ahead and provide the life he wanted for his family. He was a huge influence on me.

If my father managed to instil his work ethic into me, my mum, Anita, did her best to make me a respectful and decent human being. She's the kindest person I've ever met, and I've always wanted to make her proud. 'Mind your manners,' she liked to say when I was growing up. She taught me to treat other people the way I wanted to be treated. If I turned out well, I have her to thank for it.

Mum is Danish, so she is also responsible for my height, which has been a blessing and a curse. I had a physical advantage over other kids in footy, but I also always stood out so there was nowhere to hide. I grew 27 centimetres in my first year of school, measured by my prep teacher at the start and the end of the year. The growth spurt was so significant that I overtook most of the other students, which gave me a distinct edge on the sporting field. In games of schoolyard football with Year Fives and Sixes, I was selected as captain and ruck as early as Year Two. This was the beginning of a trend that would last throughout my school days and well into my young adult life.

I always wanted to push myself and play with the older boys. I was adamant I could perform at a higher level, and I often could, although occasionally I got into strife. I thrived on progression and I was always excessively competitive, which didn't help me fit in particularly well with a lot of people. I was always in a hurry and must have been difficult to deal with. Counterintuitively, as much as I wanted to be the best sportsman, the best student, the best at everything, I didn't enjoy the attention that came with it. I didn't like being called arrogant, just as I didn't like being left out of things or told I couldn't participate. I just wanted to get in there and get better, to be part of things.

With my parents' support, I poured that boundless energy into sport. By the time I was in Year Six, I was playing basketball for the Ringwood Hawks, the representative side for our leafy suburb in the outer east of Melbourne, as well as under-12s footy for Norwood. I had at least three games a week, plus basketball training, in a juggling act for my time and commitment. I wanted it all and I had a decent amount of talent in both sports. It was just a matter of waiting to see which one would pull ahead.

My first experience of individual recognition on the football field came when I participated in that year's Victorian Schoolboys selection process, an open competition to select a state under-12s team. It was my first real opportunity to measure myself against the best players my age, and I was desperate to make the side. The process began as an interschool event in the local area, where we played against the group of hopefuls in attendance. The first selection stage was called District and it was played at Croydon Hills. I performed well and was moved away from the ruck towards the end of the game so the selectors could see some other players. I went to full-forward, where I played against another dominant young player, Dan McStay. I didn't know him at the time, but he would become my best mate in high school, and would later be drafted into the AFL alongside me. We both made it through District and the Zone and Regional rounds, and moved on to the two final days of the selection process, which were played at the Bulleen football facilities of Trinity Grammar.

By this stage, I was turning twelve and was nearly 170 centimetres tall, which helped me on both the footy field and the basketball court. But when it came to the final days of the Victorian Schoolboys competition, it turned out to be more of a hindrance. Leading into the two-week event, which would trim the final 60 participants into a squad of 30, I was full of hope. I had performed well at every level and had no reason to believe I wouldn't do so again now.

But on the first day out, we were met with torrential rain. My boots became so heavy I could barely run, and the ball spent 99 per cent of the time skidding around on the ground, which is hardly good for a lanky, somewhat cumbersome key position player. In between games, I sheltered in the back of a car with Dan McStay and a friend of his who was a year younger than us, Christian Petracca. We joked and laughed and ate lollies to pass the time.

Despite my underwhelming performance, I somehow made it through to the following week, though to my disappointment Dan did not. We'd become quite tight through the process, and I liked having him by my side.

It rained again on the final day of the selection, and there were enormous gusts of wind. I struggled to cope with the conditions—I was all arms and legs in the mud—and I wasn't surprised at the end of the day when they told me I hadn't made the cut. The final team included a number of future AFL stars—my future housemate Josh Kelly, first-round picks Luke McDonald, Christian Salem and Jack Billings, as well as draftees Matthew Crouch, Nathan Drummond and Will Maginness. But not me. I had given my all but had come up short, and I was bitterly disappointed.

Dad met me with condolences, though it was clear that he agreed with the decision. 'You were lucky to make it through last week,' he told me.

I was shattered to hear that, but I knew it was the truth. More than anything, I was sad to have let Dad down. It felt like he had such hope going in and I hadn't lived up to it. It would be a long time before I had the chance to represent my state again.

2

COMMITMENT

Basketball consumed so much of my childhood and early teenage years that it's strange to think how fast it fell away. I started playing 'Biddy Ball' at Ringwood Basketball Centre on Friday evenings when I was five. We used to rush over after school for our 4.30 p.m. games, a rolling scrum of small kids throwing an undersized ball at an undersized hoop. It was pure fun, where dribbling the ball wasn't a priority and the referee was usually a twelve- or thirteen-year-old.

Ringwood Basketball Centre would be my home on Friday and Saturday nights for the next few years. The cold, dusty courts and the never-ending pounding of basketballs reverberating through my head was a staple of my early life. With my height and some natural talent on the court, it wasn't long before I had joined my first competitive team, Spirit Magic, in the under-8s, where my uncle Andy coached the team. 'It's all in the flick of the wrist, you've got to make the ball spin!' he told us—which turned out to be terrible advice, something we would laugh about together in later years. A few years later I joined the Ringwood Hawks, and then moved on to the Nunawading Spectres to play for a more competitive side and have a shot at playing in a state competition.

I started playing Friday nights and Saturday mornings, training midweek and on Sunday, and poor Mum was the taxi driver for most of these commitments. By my early teens, it was three basketball training sessions and two games, along-side two football training sessions and a weekly game. Our family had a house down the coast in Anglesea, and for a while Mum would drive me down there after games to meet up with Dad and my sisters, Georgia and Tessa. But in the end there were too many games, too late in the afternoon, and Mum had to sacrifice our time at the beach to meet all my sporting commitments.

Mum supported me because I was incredibly passionate about basketball, and it was a great time for us to bond—she would help the team wherever she could, and ended up as team manager for a number of seasons. In my second year with the Nunawading Spectres, we qualified for the National Club Championship in Darwin. The year after, we won the Division 2 Championship. As I was heading into the under-16s competition, the training load increased again: across footy and basketball, I had ten sports commitments a week. Something had to give.

In the under-16s, I was invited into the state team selection process for basketball, alongside a couple of my teammates. I hoped I might make the team, but I was not optimistic. Around this time, basketball became a heavier burden, not only physically but mentally and emotionally. At Nunawading, I was carrying the weight of being one of the better players on the team, and I began to train more and more in hope of making the Victorian side. The joy began to get sucked out of the sport for me as the training became more arduous and the state trials became more cut-throat.

Mum and I talked often about how I was feeling, as I think she could see that my enjoyment of the sport was waning, but we both agreed that I had invested so much in basketball that I should give it my best shot. I continued with the state trials until the final stages, when my competition for spots included the likes of Ben Simmons and Dante Exum (who have both played in the NBA), as well as Christian Petracca, another tremendous player, but ultimately I was one of the last players cut from the team.

Really, it was a blessing. Sitting in the car with Mum afterwards, I had a distinct feeling of relief. Mum asked me if I was okay.

'At least now I can focus properly on football,' I responded.

Maybe it was my ego talking, or perhaps I wanted to make my dad proud by playing the same game that he did, but a little voice in my head was telling me to play Aussie Rules. My decision to follow football was simple in the end, and final.

•

The following year, I had another chance to play football in a national competition, as part of the Victorian Metropolitan team in the 2011 AFL National Championships—if I was selected. The National Carnival would take place over approximately two weeks in the middle of the year, following a long selection process.

The first stage was to be recruited by your local representative side—mine was the Eastern Ranges—to play in the TAC Cup (now known as the NAB League). Your performance in the TAC Cup could then win you a place in a group of hopefuls who would go through a stage-by-stage selection process until, ultimately, the lucky squad of 30 were selected to represent our state. I was excited about what was ahead. I had not had the opportunity to play football at such a high level since primary school, and I dreaded missing out again.

I started my time with the Eastern Ranges in the under-16s, and things couldn't have been going better. I got along well with the coach, Mark 'Fish' Fisher, and felt he really believed in me. Likewise, regional manager Anthony Parkin, son of AFL legend David Parkin, showed a great level of confidence and care in developing me as a footballer and as a person. I had never experienced that kind of coaching before—people who struck that perfect balance of hardness and sharp feedback with true care and belief, and even a little bit of humour on the side.

The results were instant. I began to perform better than I had ever before, I moved to full-forward and found myself at home in front of goal during our limited season. A particularly good day at Victoria Park that year solidified my chances of a trial for the state side. On that day, I could do no wrong. I marked every ball, barely missed a kick and felt like I was running on top of the ground, though it wasn't the triumphant moment I'd thought it would be.

I ended the day with six or seven goals, yet in the change rooms post-game, I didn't receive the hero's welcome I was expecting. Darren Bewick, the coach of the under-18s side, waited for me to enter, pulled me aside and harangued me over a shot I'd missed in the last quarter. 'There was an easy handball right there!' he said. 'It was selfish, and I don't want to see it again!'

Immediately, my back was up. I had never even met this guy, and he was yelling at me, embarrassing me after I'd played the game of my life. I felt incredibly angry, and then upset by the ambush. *What the hell? I didn't ignore an easy handball, I was just playing on instinct . . . This guy doesn't know anything!*

'I was ten metres out,' I shot back. 'I missed an easy snap. What are you talking about?'

My reaction was visceral, and my ego was wounded. I thought I'd played the perfect game and was beyond reproach. But of course there is no such thing as a perfect game, and no one is above reproach or feedback.

This little setback aside, things were looking good for me. I continued to perform well and began training with the Vic Metro side on Tuesday nights at Princes Park, in Carlton, with the Victorian side. I immediately felt out of my comfort zone. I felt as if I were on the outer of a little club of players who had been selected to represent the state for what would be the third time in their careers. I was still training with Norwood, and still technically playing for their under-16 side, so I had the sharp contrast of moving between the state squad training and Eastern Ranges training to the familiar camaraderie of a real club. To be honest, I preferred Norwood.

Around six weeks out from the carnival, I began to have significant issues with my lower back, including pain that prevented me from bending, jumping and sprinting, so I couldn't train. I was just fifteen years old, and this was the first time I'd ever been injured, and the immediate disconnection from the playing group at both Eastern Ranges and Vic Metro hit me like a tonne of bricks. The whole rhythm of my life stopped abruptly.

Inactive for the first time ever, questions raced through

my mind. *What do I do? Why is this happening? When is it going to get better?* Unlike other injuries that have set recovery times, for my back there was no clear answer. I had my first MRI and was told that I had a protruding disc issue in my L4 and L5, which meant absolutely nothing to me. Mum informed me that this had been an issue on her side of the family, and that she'd had a discectomy after spending too much time 'picking you kids up off the floor' after one of her pregnancies.

I was full of anxious questions: 'What does this mean for the carnival? Can I train this week? What's going to fix it?' And the answer I received was the worst possible for my busy mind: 'You need to rest,' the doctor told me.

My rehab program would involve some low-level Pilates and strength work, time on the sidelines and a lot of frustration. I began to put on weight and lose conditioning, and my back didn't seem to be improving one bit. One night, I walked out of Princes Park, through the gardens close to the cemetery, and a horrible feeling of bitterness came over me.

Mum would often drive Mitch Keedle and Nick Evans home, the other Eastern Ranges players who had been selected in the Vic Metro squad, and when she asked them how training was and I heard the excitement in their voices as we approached the biggest games of our lives, while I lamely watched on from the sidelines, I felt jealousy—and then I felt guilty because of the way I felt, and became angry at myself.

I was fed up being on the sidelines. Without much improvement from the original injury, I decided I wasn't going to miss the opportunity to play in the carnival. I resolved to begin training again immediately, and to expedite my recovery process.

I was told around this time that I was to be the captain of the Victorian side that year. I had always wanted to be a captain! I loved the thought of being a good leader, as Dad had taught me. I also believed, like a lot of young people, that the captain should be the best player. If I was the captain, didn't that make me the best player? There was no way I was going to miss my moment. I was incredibly motivated to get better.

•

In 2011, the National Carnival was held in Blacktown, New South Wales, at the excellent facilities newly built for the GWS Giants. I will never forget walking into that vast, shining facility—I was awestruck. I couldn't believe how big everything was. Silly as it may seem, what stood out most was that I had never seen a net as big as the one built behind the goalposts to stop balls flying into the car park— it seemed like an impossible feat of human ingenuity. The National Carnival finally felt real—and unbelievably daunting.

In the official guide to the 2011 National Championships,

I was recorded at 196 centimetres tall and 105 kilograms in weight, making me the biggest kid there by a stretch. Players from all states stayed at the same hotel, and multiple times over the first couple of days players from other sides came to see if there was really a 105-kilogram fifteen-year-old. This made me uncomfortable. I hated the feeling that I was different or strange or freakish.

These feelings were compounded by my initial performances on the field, which were disappointing. *I've let everyone down*, I thought. *I'm the captain—I've got to play well and lead from the front.* The pressure got to me and the guilt began to pile up.

In one game, I missed a rudimentary snap at goal and my opposition immediately attacked the miss. 'Hungry,' he sneered. 'All about you, is it?'

His words cut straight through me. *Should I have handballed? Was I being selfish?* I couldn't do that—I was the captain. For some reason, that moment made me feel like more of a failure in my own head than I had ever felt before.

A guest speaker came to talk to us while we were at dinner one night at the hotel, a former Vic Metro captain named Alex Johnson, who had been drafted by the Sydney Swans. I immediately saw myself in him. We were both captains, and he was from the Oakleigh Chargers and I was from the Eastern Ranges, which was as geographically as close as we could get. He spoke about the challenges of the AFL, his first preseason and some of his experiences as a footballer. But the thing that stood out most was when he spoke about seizing opportunities. He talked about the importance of playing well in front of the recruiters, and how we were all lucky to be where we were.

'Don't let this chance pass you by,' he said. 'That one outstanding performance can be enough to propel your career forward.'

The more Alex spoke, the more I shrivelled up, and the more guilt I felt about my poor performances in the carnival. As the games continued, his words rang in my head: *Don't let it slip . . . you only need one great game.* I should have learned from what Alex had to say about leadership, about overcoming adversity, about the challenges ahead—but instead I focused on me, myself, my performance.

I didn't have that great game, in the end. I had moments, flashes of my talent, but ultimately left the tournament shattered. The Australian team was selected, and any flicker of hope I had that others believed in me more than I believed in myself was crushed when my name was not on the list.

Returning to my Eastern Ranges teammates, my schoolmates and my family, I was forced to have some of the hardest conversations I could imagine. Enthusiastically, they would ask, 'How was it? How did you go?'

Every question was a dagger to my ego. I could only shrug and say, 'Alright,' or make up some excuse about my injury, or talk about how it was hard playing with players from other teams. It felt like they had all watched the vision from my games, seen my disappointing performances and were just trying to rub it in. Salt in my wounds.

I questioned at that point whether I wanted to continue with football—whether I had made the right decision in leaving basketball behind. I was sure my former basketball teammates and their parents were now laughing at my failure. I had made a grand gesture of choosing my path and had been so sure it was going to work out. All of a sudden it felt like I had made a big mistake.

There was one redeeming thing about that year, something for which I would be eternally grateful. Dad coached me, for the last time, in the under-16s at Norwood.

Before the season started, he asked me straight out, 'Are you going to be able to deal with me being your coach again?' I was adamant that it was a good idea—after all, a couple of key things had changed in recent times. Firstly, I had grown up a lot. Dad and I had developed a strong level of respect over the previous couple of years, and I was far more driven, professional and more capable of taking feedback— or so I thought. Secondly, I knew my time at Norwood was limited because of the TAC Cup and the National Carnival— I was only likely to play enough games for Norwood to qualify for finals.

But most importantly, what Dad and I had felt like a partnership. He had begun to ask me for input on a range of different coaching topics. 'What do you think about playing him on the wing?' he'd say. 'Have you been doing any good drills at Eastern that we could do here?' I felt valued and, because of that, I played my heart out for him.

The Norwood under-16s fell short of a premiership that year, getting knocked out in the preliminary final on a miserable day in Knox, but I shared some really special moments with Dad that season. As the stakes in my football career started to rise, and as I began feeling the pressure of that, I was grateful for the simplicity and comfort that he brought to the game.

3

RECOGNITION

After my time at Norwood came to a close, I was full of excitement because I was entering my first full season with the TAC Cup squad at Eastern Ranges. I was eager to get started, to leave the disappointment of the 2011 National Carnival behind me and prove that I was one of the best young players in the country.

Our training cycle kicked off with a camp at a YMCA in Queenscliff in November 2011: a gruelling three-day program of physical activities, football training and football education. I had barely finished the last footy season before the next one got started—the first preseason of many in the coming years.

When we arrived at camp, we started by getting our measurements done—height, weight and skinfolds. I had never done a skinfold test and I really didn't know what to expect, so I wasn't particularly worried about it. When the team's high performance coach plucked at my belly fat with a pair of pincers and read out the number—'Eighty-four'—it meant nothing to me. But he clearly thought it was a problem. The coach laughed and remarked, loudly enough for the twenty young players behind me to hear, 'Geez, you've got some work to do.'

Shame settled on my fifteen-year-old shoulders like a fully loaded barbell. I was so embarrassed. *Is 84 bad? Does that mean I'm fat? Does that mean I can't play?* I was completely pulled apart by his comment. I'd gone into the training on such a high, and now I felt like I had fallen at the first hurdle.

I spent the remainder of the camp avoiding 'bad food', having half-meals and trying to shed the extra fat in the course of three days. It was a hopeless mission. I couldn't lose the fat overnight, but I began to develop an anxiety about my weight that would last until the end of my playing career.

In the weeks leading up to Christmas, I trained harder, starting earlier and finishing later than most of my team-mates. I would finish the scheduled training session at Kilsyth Recreation Reserve and would immediately join Dad for an extra goalkicking session at Norwood. The two of us would take turns to fetch the ball, kick after kick, until I felt I had perfected it for the evening. Then I would head inside to do an extensive upper-body and lower-body weights session, trying to increase my strength. I was squatting in excess of 150 kilograms, and running kilometres every day.

The team broke for Christmas that year around the middle of December, but I had no intention of slowing down. The shame of being a 'fat' footy player drove me nonstop that summer, and losing kilos became my main focus in preparing for the season ahead. My family decamped to our house in Anglesea, as we did every year, but it wasn't the usual calm, rejuvenating holiday for me. I was consumed by worries about what was to come. I filled my summer days with running sessions, weights sessions at the Anglesea Football Club gym, and swimming sessions at the pool.

Every session I did in Anglesea—by myself or with some coaching from Dad—was a solitary grind that left me longing for the return of scheduled training, so I would have the energy of a team around me. But I felt stronger by the end of the summer, and I returned for the first training session after the break eager and ready to put myself to work. I was going to blow them away with how much I had improved. I would increase my workload and training levels with the team, and convince anyone who doubted me that my best was yet to come.

The very first training session back involved a two-kilometre time trial, designed to check everyone's fitness levels following the time off. Before we got started, the high performance coach for Eastern, a guy called Sean Murphy, insisted we all put our runners on for the trial, but I hadn't brought any.

'What do you mean you don't have any runners?' he asked, perplexed.

I had come straight from school and had only brought my football boots. 'Don't worry, I'll just run in these,' I responded.

It was an extremely hot evening, and by the halfway point my mouth was dry, my feet were throbbing and I was soaked in sweat, but I crossed the finish line in a time of seven minutes and 30 seconds—faster than I had done at any point over the summer. I was satisfied that I had improved, and I sought out Sean to chat with him about it. I needed validation for my work.

'How'd I go?' I asked eagerly, hoping for some praise.

'You've still got a lot of work to do, mate,' he replied.

I couldn't believe it. Again I was cut to pieces. I couldn't understand it. I was training well, being professional and dedicated, and my football was improving every session, yet these numbers were making me feel like a failure. Some of my teammates were walking around proudly after running faster, lifting heavier weights or recording lower skinfolds, but somehow I was still getting it wrong. I was still not good enough.

I became more and more concerned about my weight and fitness. It felt like a huge black mark on my copybook to not be as fit or as lean as some of the other players—it was as though they had some special badge of honour that I lacked.

'Mum, I need to lose some weight,' I complained. 'What can I do?'

'Well, you could start with not eating Sustain twice a day!' she answered.

I was a teenager; I didn't really understand nutrition. If not eating cereal would help, I figured, then surely skipping lunch would be even better. I began to cut down my food consumption dramatically. I wasn't looking for a sustainable diet, I was looking for fast results. I began bringing food home from school—and when Mum noticed that, I started throwing it out at lunchtime. Then I skipped food at recess too, and my energy levels started fading throughout the day. I would eat something small for lunch, and then follow it up with a heap of water to help me feel full.

During the school holidays, it was harder to starve myself. I had a lot more spare time—which meant more chances to notice how hungry I was. The feedback kept coming at Eastern Ranges, and it was more of the same: I was 'too slow', 'too heavy', like a lumbering baby. I felt like people thought my size and shape had been an advantage in junior footy— the reason for my success to date—but that I had reached the ceiling of my potential. I was going to prove them wrong.

●

If there was one thing that made the year a bit brighter, it was my mate Dan McStay. Preseason training with Eastern Ranges was three nights a week, and it was a strain on my parents to get me there. Both Mum and Dad were working at that stage. My younger sister Tessa was playing more and more basketball with the Nunawading Spectres, and our schedules were making our parents' lives a logistical nightmare.

In previous years, I had gone to a family friend's house after school to eat, get changed and prepare for training, while Mum raced over from her work at Mont Albert Primary School to pick me up and get me to training in the nick of time. But this all changed when Dan was selected alongside me at the Eastern Ranges and we started training together.

I had started high school wearing a moon boot—the result of a basketball injury—and with no friends, but Dan quickly became one of my absolute best. Actually, first of all we got into a fistfight, wrestling each other to the dirt right in front of the staff room, but after that he became my best mate.

I can't remember what we fought about, but I know why we became friends. We were in most of the same classes and shared most of the same interests. We did Maths Methods, English, Physics and Further Maths together, and we spent lunchtime playing downball with a huge group of boys, alongside the basketball stadium.

Our downball games started out innocently enough, but in our later years of high school the competitiveness really ramped up. We started organising rankings and end-of-term tournaments that drew huge crowds from around the school. We took it far too seriously, and it led to a few challenges with teachers, not to mention arguments among our friends. Dan and I were among the top seeds in our downball fraternity (honourable mentions also go to Andy Moore, Mark Presser and Mitch Daniels). I continually wore a hole in the front side of my right school shoe playing downball, much to the dismay of my mother, who could not understand why it was happening.

The other great passion Dan and I shared was football. Three nights a week, Dan's parents, Deb and Trev, would feed us and drive us to training at Eastern Ranges, showing extraordinary generosity. Dan and I absolutely loved it—we could spend more time together, hanging out for an hour or so after school, talking footy, watching Foxtel (which was a real treat for me) or chatting with his parents. As much as my football career had its challenges that year, I really enjoyed feeling a part of something with Dan and his parents.

•

The pressure definitely mounted around the TAC Cup. After my unremarkable performance the year before, I was eager to make my mark at the top level for Victorian junior footballers. The game was tougher and it was a significant shift from the football I had played at Norwood, but I quickly found my feet and recognised the advantages of playing at a higher level.

Gone were the days of playing on small, muddy ovals with poor facilities; the grandstands were suddenly stadiums. The small ovals of the eastern suburbs became the vast expanses of Princes Park, Kardinia Park and Box Hill City Oval. We had new footballs to play and train with—I couldn't believe the difference that using good footballs had on consistency in training, skills and games. The style of play was more open, because with bigger grounds came more space, and the higher skill level meant the ball moved much faster. The quality of players across the board meant that there were few, if any, who didn't possess one outstanding athletic quality or another.

The increase in professionalism trickled down to all facets of my footballing life: training was longer, more specific and more challenging. We spent more time analysing our individual and team performances, reinforcing what worked, breaking down what didn't and planning how to improve. Of course, not all the changes were good. As a junior footballer, I had always been in successful teams, winning lightning premierships with the under-11s, as well as two premierships at Norwood. In fact, I had never played a season without making finals, but that wasn't the case in my first season with Eastern Ranges.

We began the year at Princes Park against the Oakleigh Chargers, with high hopes but no real idea of where we sat in the competition. In a relatively spirited affair, we ended up going down by 28 points. I played well, kicking two goals, and was pleased with my individual performance. My fitness was significantly better than it had been in preseason, and I felt confident in my ability and comfortable among players who were generally a year or two older than me.

In our next game, we played the Northern Knights, but after a promising first half we were blown out of the water and went down by 57 points. Yet I'd played my best game to date—I kicked six goals—so the loss left me with mixed feelings. In the rooms after the game, I thought to myself, *Should I be happy that I played well, after we lost by ten goals?* I had never encountered this dilemma before, because I had always played in winning teams. It was uncomfortable.

As the season continued, the losses kept piling up. A 67-point loss to the Western Jets was followed by our second-worst loss for the year, a 100-point drubbing by the Sandringham Dragons. We would reach the end of Round 7 having lost every game, by an average of 64 points.

It bothered me that the team was doing so badly, but I was comforted by my own strong performances. It gave me a sense of focus and allowed me to overcome the general mood of failure surrounding the club at the time. I felt vindicated, too, for all the extra work I had put in. I was a standout player, and not because I was overweight or unfit. I was just playing well. I kicked 22 goals across the first seven games we played, with hauls of four, five and six goals. Then we came up against the only other side that had been struggling as much as us, the Bendigo Pioneers. We prepared as though it was a final.

Unfortunately, we had to play at the Pioneers' home ground—in Bendigo, obviously—which meant a couple of hours in the car, driving into enemy territory. The Pioneers also had one of the most talked about players in our age group at the time, Jake Stringer, who had returned from a broken leg a few weeks earlier and kicked ten goals in a game. It was hard to imagine winning at that point. Our hopes of playing in the finals had been crushed by our seven bad losses, and in the lead-up to the game we spoke grimly about 'finding some meaning in our year'.

We played well in a game that was full of emotion, scuffles and physicality. I performed well, but so did my team, and we got to sing our song for the first time that year after a 28-point victory. It was such a satisfying feeling. The stars had aligned for us: the weather had been perfect for a game in June, the ground was in good condition and we all played well (for once!). It felt like a miracle.

On the long drive home with Dad after the game, I was glowing. It felt great to have stuck at something when our hopes and aspirations seemed lost. For it to have paid off in the form of a victory felt amazing. I knew Dad was proud of me. He hated losing, and I think watching the team struggle while I tried to build my profile as a young footballer was difficult for him, though he never said as much.

•

My relationship with Dad changed dramatically over that year. When I was younger, I felt like a child around him, because I was young and immature. In my final year at Norwood and into my first season at Eastern Ranges, I felt myself starting to become his equal. He treated me with respect, and I was extremely appreciative of the insights he gave me on my game, since he watched me more closely than anyone.

After some of the bad losses at Eastern, I often walked away with the attitude that it wasn't my fault: *I did what I needed to do.* Dad never let me get away with that. He reinforced to me the things I could have done better: 'You didn't jump as freely for your marks today . . . Did you cover as much ground today?'

My response was usually defensive: 'It's hard to run when the ball is always in our backline . . .'

That wasn't good enough for Dad. 'You always have to find a way,' he would reply.

We began developing a push/pull relationship that worked much better for me than just being told what to do. I stopped blaming others for my failures as much as I had done previously, particularly at the National Carnival the year before, and began focusing on what I could improve, regardless of the outcome of a game. Dad's 'criticism' became 'feedback' in my mind, and was much more palatable because he made concessions for my performances when the circumstances of the game were dire. Yet he would always hold me accountable for my attitude, perseverance and commitment across four quarters.

•

With the strength of my performance in the TAC Cup competition, I had caught the eye of the selectors for the Victorian Metro team, who were once again recruiting for the National Carnival. After the disappointment of the 2011 carnival, I was more determined than ever to prove that I was good enough to play at state level, and I used it as motivation to perform well through the tougher times that Eastern Ranges was having.

By mid-2012, I had gone through the same selection process I had the year before, and was training on Tuesdays with the Vic Metro team in Carlton and on Thursdays with Ranges in Kilsyth. I was one of only three players from Eastern to be selected for Vic Metro. Luckily for me, the other two both had their driver's licence. So either Brandon Wood (the captain of Eastern Ranges that year) or Mitch O'Donnell (everyone called him Bully) would pick me up from school and drive me to state training each week.

Walking into Princes Park for the first training session that year, I felt way out of my depth. In the room were players from the 2011 All-Australian team, young men who would go on to be first-round draft picks later in the year. Joe Daniher, Kristian Jaksch, Aidan Corr, Lachie Plowman and the captain, Nick Vlastuin, were all there, chatting easily with each other. Wood, Bully and I seemed conspicuous as the three boys from the eastern suburbs, and it took me a while to feel like I fitted in. Eventually I made friends with a couple of other players, including Nathan Hrovat and Jack Macrae, who made an effort to spend time with me and helped me feel more at home.

Before long, we were preparing for the first game of the National Carnival, an exciting trip north to play in Darwin against the Northern Territory Thunder. Jumping off the plane, I was struck by the imposing heat and humidity that is Darwin weather in the middle of winter, and I immediately felt slightly less confident about our chances. The unfamiliar teammates, the oppressive conditions and the exotic location had me thinking back to the 2011 carnival and my own disappointing effort.

Over the next two days, while preparing for the game, my mind was racing. *What if I play badly? I have to kick some goals. What if my teammates don't kick me the ball?* Mindless thought after mindless thought, all about me, myself and I.

Game day arrived, and I was met with yet another curveball: we were playing a night game and it was hot, sweaty and slippery. From the first bounce I felt lethargic, nervous and worried, completely out of sorts. I dropped an easy mark early, then missed an easy shot on goal. *Not again!* I was filled with the same despair that had consumed me the year before. I wasn't alone—many of my teammates were struggling to get a handle on the conditions and the game, and there were fumbles, skill errors and missed tackles everywhere.

To add to our woe, the crowd was much bigger than anticipated and extremely vocal. I would later learn that people had travelled from far and wide to Darwin to watch the game. I couldn't believe the skill level of the Thunder that night, the speed, the talent. Some extraordinary goals were kicked; they demonstrated a sheer brilliance with the ball that was greater than anything I'd seen. They played with spirit, hunger and desire, all of which we lacked. I felt as though I was a spectator on the ground—I certainly played like it—and we became the first Victorian team to lose to the Northern Territory since the competition began.

I walked into our change rooms with my head down. I was shattered. I wanted to crawl into a hole and never come out. *I've completely failed, again.* The team was delivered some extremely frank criticism by our coach, Rohan Welsh. 'For many of you, that was your one and only chance to represent your state,' he said. 'Before the game, I told you to respect the Big V, respect the jumper, and you didn't do that tonight.'

He went around the room and gave each and every one of us a stern review; only a few players who had done their job were spared: Nick Vlastuin and Jack Macrae had performed admirably. I hid in the corner until I thought the spray was over, but then I felt a tap on the shoulder. Anton Grbac, the program manager, took me and three of my teammates aside to receive another round of criticism.

To my confusion, the feedback wasn't about my performance, which had been abysmal. 'I don't care if you don't get a kick or drop a mark, Tom, but it's unacceptable to drop your head and start thinking about yourself,' Anton said. It was my attitude and not my mistakes that drew his anger. I stewed on this for the next 24 hours.

Many of the better Vic Metro players had not been required to play the game in Darwin, as the team managers were trying to showcase as much of the squad as possible to the various AFL clubs' recruiting staff. Walking into training the following Tuesday, I was filled with dread: we had let those players down and hurt their chances for a carnival win. 'What happened?' they wanted to know. I didn't know what to say.

I was sure my time with the Vic Metro team wouldn't last long after that—I expected to be told that my services were no longer required, and that I wouldn't play the next game, against Tasmania. I would return to Eastern Ranges from the state side for the second time in as many years as a huge disappointment, an embarrassment.

But Anton approached me after training and, to my huge surprise, said, 'Tommy, we are going to stick with you this week. I know you didn't play well but we want to see you bounce back.'

I was shocked. *They still believed in me?* I felt elated, and absolutely determined to do the right thing by Anton—to justify his faith in me. Suddenly, it wasn't about me anymore: I was playing to prove Anton right, and to help my team win.

I had a slightly different role in the game that week, playing ruck against one of the biggest ruckmen in the country. It was a cold day at Princes Park, but in contest after contest I stayed present, smashing into the opposition ruckman, pushing forward where I could, tackling hard, blocking and trying to make a positive impact. I was determined not to drop my head.

It wasn't my best game ever, but I was proud of my effort. I had held up my end of the bargain. I had proven—to the coaches and to myself—that I was good enough to play at the top level.

•

I had a weird feeling following the game against Tasmania, which we won. I was pleased that I had improved, but with the two games against the weaker football states behind us, I suspected that I hadn't done enough to be selected for the remaining matches.

I was hopeful throughout that week—I trained well, I was more bubbly and talkative with my teammates—but my fears were soon realised. Rohan Welsh approached me and said, 'Boydie, we were much happier with your performance on the weekend. I thought your ruckwork was really good.' I could feel a 'but' coming, and sure enough it did. 'But we aren't going to take you to Adelaide this weekend. We want you to go back and play at TAC Cup. Play well—you are still a part of this.'

I was so disheartened. My thoughts were racing, but I kept them to myself. *I just need one more chance . . . I know I'm close to having a great game. What about him? He played worse than me.* But even as I complained to myself, I heard Anton's voice berating me: 'Don't drop your head!' It felt like a test to see how I handled bad news, and I wasn't going to fail this time.

I stopped feeling sorry for myself, and I went out and trained. I was the loudest, hardest-training, most engaged version of myself I could be. I refused to show any sign of disappointment, bitterness or jealousy. I bottled all those emotions up, trained the house down and kept my disappointment to myself—until I jumped in the car with Mum. I told her the news, then didn't say a word for the rest of the drive home.

•

The game for Eastern that weekend was the one in Bendigo—the first game that we won all season. After not having trained with the team much at all for the past few weeks, I was excited to be there, back and comfortable in my own domain with my own teammates. I played the way I knew I could, marking strongly, kicking straight and enjoying the freedom of playing with Ranges again.

I returned to Vic Metro training the next Tuesday, with no expectations but with my head held high. I was proud of my performance and eager to chat to my teammates, who had played and won a great game in South Australia. After training, I was told that I was required again on Thursday night, which was the norm for the players who were being considered for the game that weekend. I would only be an emergency, I was sure. If I didn't get picked for the Vic Metro side I wouldn't be playing at all that weekend, as Eastern had a bye.

Anton pulled me aside for a chat at the Thursday training session, and we walked around the oval together. Every time he looked at me, the dread that had lingered from our interaction in Darwin rushed back.

'You played well on the weekend, Tom,' he said.

'Yeah, I was okay,' I said. 'It was good to get a win.'

Anton followed up quickly: 'No, you played well. You must have been disappointed but you didn't drop your head, you went back and played the way you needed to, and from all reports made the difference on the day.' He continued, 'You know, we watch you just as much playing TAC Cup as we do here. Some of your teammates had poor games and played with poor attitudes after being put in the same position as you. So we are going to play you again this week.'

I was startled. 'Thanks,' I said, but that was all. I was barely able to control my excitement, and words had left me.

'You deserve it,' Anton finished. 'Now go on.'

I had another chance. We were playing Vic Country at Kardinia Park in Geelong, one of my favourite grounds.

The lead-up to the game was exciting. Fox Footy was broadcasting it and there were cameras everywhere—players were even being interviewed on television before the first bounce! That was new. I could barely keep my nerves in check, yet even so—and unlike any of my previous state games—I was feeling settled in the team. I had spent more time with these teammates now, and become more comfortable with them. I knew I deserved to be there. I had played well at Kardinia Park before, and the conditions were perfect for a weekend in June: windy but dry, no nasty surprises.

From the first bounce, I was in the zone. The early play filled me with confidence, and in the second half I got my chance to make an impact, kicking three goals and taking some big marks to help us get across the line 8.18 (66) to 6.15 (51).

After the game, I couldn't quite comprehend what had happened. In two short weeks I had gone from desperate disappointment to burgeoning young gun—and suddenly we were one win away from being crowned national champions. Players congratulated me in the rooms, laughing and hugging, many of them knowing how challenging the last couple of weeks had been for me.

Rohan smiled and patted me on the back, and Anton gave me a wicked grin as he approached, laughing and shaking my hand. 'That's more like it!' he said.

I felt like I had finally arrived at the top level, and I couldn't wipe the grin off my face for days.

•

Training the following week was a joy. For the first time, I was the player in the Vic Metro team to be jealous of, whose performance was to be envied. I had shot onto the draft radar for the following year and was the talk of the National Carnival. It felt like players respected me more, were more talkative with me and even friendlier. I felt like I belonged.

Our final game was against Western Australia and was played at Docklands, my first game at the indoor venue. Vic Country would play South Australia in the game before us, and if South Australia won, we would have to win to become national champions and retain the title for Vic Metro. We eagerly watched the first game play out and the South Australians won, as anticipated, although the margin was just thirteen points.

The final was my first game playing alongside highly touted father-son draft prospect Joe Daniher, and I was nervous about how well we would work together. From the beginning of the match it was clear to me why Joe was so highly regarded. He moved quickly, demanded the ball, jumped aggressively and marked better than anyone I had ever seen.

We scored nine goals to two in the first half and things seemed almost certain to go our way, though it was a tightly fought second half. Ultimately, we won by 24 points and secured the National Championship. I played well, as a ruck/forward, and was named one of the best players in the match. I didn't get anywhere near as much attention as I had the week before, but that was okay. I had the following year to look forward to, and I had already proven myself.

•

I returned to Eastern Ranges, where our confidence was the highest it had been that year, to play at Box Hill City Oval against the Geelong Falcons. I kicked five goals in a best-on-ground performance, as we won by 31 points. The next week we had a tight, twelve-point win against the Calder Cannons at what had to be the windiest ground in Victoria, Highgate Reserve in Craigieburn.

After three good wins, it felt like we were back on track for the remainder of the season. We had found some good form, and some of our players had stepped up to perform really well. Unfortunately, the remaining seven rounds would be like the first seven—all losses. Adding another notch to the losing column each week made it more difficult for me to find joy in the game, particularly when all of our losses but one were by over 30 points.

I tried to focus on performing well individually, but even that was becoming more difficult. More and more attention was being paid to me by opposition teams and defenders, and I often experienced double team defence as well as physical and verbal scuffles, all intended to throw me off my game.

I found myself facing an internal challenge as well, struggling to answer my own question: *What are we even playing for?* I wanted to feel pride in my performance, that wasn't an issue. I loved playing well, even in losing sides. But as the year wore on, I felt the need to attach meaning to each game in order to find the intensity I needed to play well in less than favourable conditions, or against strong opponents. With finals no longer on the cards, I had to work hard to salvage some sense of purpose.

A large proportion of our team was still early in their TAC Cup experience—sometimes as many as seventeen of the 22 players on game day. That meant many of us were destined to spend another year in the underage competition before we became eligible for the AFL's National Draft, so we had the following season to try to improve our prospects. It didn't seem likely that many, if any, of our older teammates would be drafted at the end of the year. We knew that if we played well, it would give them the best chance of being selected by an AFL club, but it was hard to use that as a motivating factor.

Instead, some of the more senior bottom-age players, such as Mitch Honeychurch, Ben Cavarra and I, made a concerted effort to consolidate our skills for the following season. We knew that we could use the final games of our bottom-age year to propel ourselves individually, and to propel our team into better performances. If we couldn't win, that at least gave us some purpose and direction for the remaining games.

●

We finished at the bottom of the 2012 TAC Cup ladder, with just three wins and fourteen losses. At the end of the season, I was invited to the awards ceremony at Docklands, where I won the award as the competition's leading goal-kicker and was named centre half-forward in the TAC Cup's Team of the Year.

Considering the way my team had performed that year, it was pleasing to be recognised, and it occurred to me that sometimes it was easier to be seen if you were playing well individually in a poor team. I had always felt jealous of other players in the competition who played well in good sides, particularly the forwards. *Imagine how good I could be if we won every week!* But in a way I was able to leverage Eastern's poor performance, both for added validation and as an excuse for my own shortcomings. I was always able to say, 'Well, it's pretty tough trying to kick goals with only twenty inside-50s a game and losing by twelve goals!' But on the other hand, when I played well I could say, 'Imagine how many goals I could kick if we were actually good!'

As the year had progressed, I had become more and more obsessed with my individual performance as a player, and I knew that no real validation of success was going to come from the team as we toiled away at the bottom of the ladder. But I struggled to know how I ranked against others, or if I was improving, and I would spend a lot of time and energy comparing myself to others. Personal accolades like being selected in the Team of the Year gave me confidence that I had a future in football.

Over the course of 2012, more and more attention had been coming my way. Scouts had been showing up at my games for a couple of years, but that was pretty standard in junior football. Now, though, it wasn't just scouts but suddenly media people, journalists, cameras. For the first time in my life, at barely seventeen years old, I started to hear my name coming out of the mouths of people I had never met, and all of them were speculating about my future football career. It was very strange.

My friends at school started to know my results and my stats even before I did, as websites that follow AFL draft hopefuls began to follow my career more intently. I received requests for interviews, managers began to send me letters of interest, and strangers at local football games stopped me for a chat. All this attention felt new and exciting, but it was difficult to process. It was difficult to wrap my head around the idea that I was *someone* to people I didn't know.

The attention surrounding my TAC Cup games was one thing, but the attention I began to receive at local games, at school and in public was something else. During the season, I would often go with Dad to watch Norwood's senior side play, but it became more difficult for us to watch the games uninterrupted. Local supporters, well-wishers and football lovers sought me out, asking me questions and talking about my recent games or speculating about my future. I had known some of them for a long time, but now they were paying me a lot more attention.

The first time I was asked to take a photo with someone was on a cold Saturday afternoon at Mullum Mullum Reserve, by a young kid who played juniors with Norwood. We were surrounded by club supporters, including people I had grown up with, and I was overwhelmed with embarrassment. The last thing I wanted was for people to think I had a big head.

Dad and I began to watch the game from the far side of the oval after that, avoiding as much interaction as possible. I was there to support the players and watch the game, not to draw attention to myself. I didn't feel like I had changed at all, but in many people's eyes I was no longer the kid playing in the mud at half time.

In a way, I enjoyed the attention because it validated my talent, and the improvements I'd made, but I didn't enjoy the impositions on my life. I wanted the interest but not the interaction. I wanted to succeed, but I didn't want the scrutiny.

•

With my bottom-age TAC Cup year behind me, I was confident I was only twelve months away from being an AFL footballer. I had the height, the athleticism, the skills and an array of strong performances behind me. I knew that, in Victoria at least, I was beginning to set myself apart. Key position players who performed as well as I had were few and far between, and the focus in my mind had changed from if I was going to be drafted to where. This thrilled me. I was now gunning to be the best key forward not only in Victoria, but in the whole country.

I set my sights on being the number 1 pick in the AFL National Draft in 2013, and I used that prospect to motivate me. I was determined, but still hadn't convinced myself yet. I wanted it to be undeniable, to myself and to others, that I was the best player in the draft. I read comparisons between myself and players who'd been drafted in 2012—including Joe Daniher and Jesse Hogan—and players drafted previously, like Jon Patton. I had real doubts that I was better than these players—particularly Joe, as I'd seen him perform acts on the football field that I never had—but my competitive drive kicked in.

After the hype surrounding the draft in 2012, I struggled to take pleasure in other people's success, particularly those who were selected in my position. I didn't feel impatient to be drafted, I felt impatient to prove that I was the best. I began obsessing over it, pouring my life and my self-esteem into this imaginary system of ranking, this purely speculative competition about a draft order that was still twelve months away. I had a year to convince myself and everyone else that I was as good as I hoped I was.

I wasn't playing football for fun anymore. With the most important season of my life ahead of me, I was playing for my career.

4

DRESS REHEARSAL

Much like the year earlier, my time down at Anglesea over the summer was far from idyllic. The summers of my childhood had been filled with sand, sun and surf, but I went back that year to running at the oval, strength sessions and swimming sessions. The hot days were filled with routine and structure.

When I was young, it always felt like summer finished too soon—like I was holding on to every last second, every moment, until our family returned to Ringwood, to school and the rest of regular life. It always felt like those summer days slipped away too quickly. Now my focus was firmly fixed on the future. The dread of another running session, done alone in the oppressive heat, led me to wish the summer away. I wanted it to be over. Anglesea was no longer carefree: it was where I was preparing for my final year of junior football, for Year 12 and for the National Draft. With so much riding on the next ten months, I found it impossible to relax.

The president of the local footy club—best known by his nickname, 'Mongrel'—kindly gave me access to the gym there so I could complete my program from Eastern Ranges, which I would most often do after a long session of running and skills practice at Ellimatta Reserve.

When I was younger, I was always trying to keep up with Dad—trying to run as fast as him, kick as far and be as strong. But now I had caught up to him, both in fitness and in football skills, so his role as my unofficial summer coach had become as exhausting for him as it was for me. We would run and kick together, wrestle in marking contests, and he would stand the mark while I practised goalkicking. He wasn't the fit young man he used to be, but he did his best.

We went through this process every second day for the entire summer, getting up early to run to avoid the heat, following up with a gym session when we could get a key or doing bodyweight exercises on the oval if we couldn't. Dad would drive me to Waurn Ponds on our off-days for a pool session, or I would swim the bay at Point Roadknight, when the ocean conditions allowed.

It wasn't all serious. I still swam and surfed when I could, and did my best to enjoy the time away, but I had to keep my priorities clear. I had to train first, then I had to get a head start on my Year 12 schoolwork, then I was free. I knew I had my work cut out for me to get a good score in Maths Methods, though I'd always been good at maths. It had become apparent to me in Year 11 that Methods required serious work—I couldn't just coast and expect to do well. For my English class I was reading David Malouf's novel *Ransom*, based on the ancient Greek story of the fall of Troy, and the defeat of the Trojans by the Greeks and the great warrior Achilles.

I could feel the pressures of adult life kicking in. I had been a kid with endless time up to that point, but now I realised that everything counted. There were no second chances, and the results I got in school and in football that year would be something I'd have to live with forever.

Two or three weeks before I returned to preseason training at Eastern Ranges, I began to feel the same creeping uncertainty about my fitness. Had I done enough work? Was I lean enough? *I shouldn't have missed that session . . . What are my skinfolds at the moment?* Quickly, the uncertainty became dread and I began to wish I could fast-forward a few weeks, skipping the measurements and the time trials. I wanted to jump ahead to the point where all that mattered was your performance on the training track.

•

Along with my school homework that summer, I had a significant bit of football homework to do: I had to pick a manager. The journey in selecting a manager had been a strange one up to that point. I received my first letter from a management company in 2011, a bonus of being selected in the state side. It was an exciting moment, and a point of pride among the players at Eastern Ranges. But in the eighteen months that followed, I received dozens of letters from different companies courting me, and I quickly realised that, apart from the name at the top, the letters were identical from player to player. The thrill died away after that.

I talked at length to Eastern's regional manager, Anthony Parkin, about it and decided that finding a management company was a necessary evil. 'Parko' discouraged players from signing too soon with managers. 'I've seen too many players get smoke blown up their arse by managers and not get drafted,' he told me. 'Better to take your time and keep your feet on the ground.' There was an almost combative relationship between TAC clubs and the management companies, and I sensed that Parko was trying to protect his players for as long as possible.

Dad and I spoke about it frequently, and together we decided that it was in my best interests to pick someone that summer and get it out of the way. The frequent enquiries were distractions—just another thing I needed to juggle. We felt certain I would be drafted somewhere, and I didn't feel that I would be influenced negatively by management one way or another, so I just wanted to get it over with.

So as 2012 came to an end, I sifted through the pile of letters that had accumulated over the past couple of years and came up with a shortlist of people to speak to, three managers that I connected with in one way or another.

'Don't forget that they work for you, Tom,' Dad reminded me. With that in mind, we conducted the meetings with each management company like job interviews. My first meeting was with Scott Lucas, an Essendon superstar whom I greatly admired, who worked for a company called Phoenix. We spoke about his current clients, brand partners and potential sponsorship offerings.

What became clear was that, unlike in those movies where managers offer their players huge deals in their first meetings, for young AFL players performance had to come first. This shifted my mindset, because now I was picking based on the person, and not on a commercial opportunity. I sat quietly for much of the meeting, slowly coming into the conversation as I felt more comfortable, and grateful to have Dad by my side. I left the meeting certain that Scott was the one.

Dad was always the voice of reason. 'Just settle down, Tom,' he told me. 'He was good, but we have nothing to compare it to.'

Next on the list was Adam Ramanauskas, from ESP, and my immediate impression of him was also good. He'd prepared a well-constructed slide deck for us to look at and I could tell he meant business. It was obvious that ESP was a much bigger company than Phoenix, and had a long track record of managing high-profile players and sponsors.

I was certain once again. 'What do you reckon about that one, Dad?' I asked.

'I think he was better, but we still have another company to talk to,' Dad replied.

My excitement and impatience were obvious, but Dad remained objective and conducted the process professionally. Last on the list was Paul Connors, from Connors Management. He was a well-known face to me as I had met him several times at TAC Cup and state games, which he often attended. The meeting was the most comfortable by far. We chatted freely, he was very professional and we had a good rapport.

For the third time in a row, I walked out certain that this was the right choice—and for the third time Dad dampened my excitement. 'There's one more I want you to meet before we decide,' he told me. Geoff Lisle, one of Dad's best mates, had recommended an agent called Liam Pickering.

I wasn't particularly excited by the proposition. *Not another one*, I thought. The meetings were long and tiring, they took a lot of emotional and mental energy to prepare for and the process had already dragged out for over a month by that stage. Even so, I agreed to meet with him. Like all the ones before, I thought the meeting went very well, better than any of the others.

That was definitely the end of the line. We let everyone know that we would make a decision in January.

•

Having completed that process, I was glad to have it out of the way. I couldn't imagine going through it during the season, with both school and football at their peak. Dad and I spoke at length a number of times over summer about which direction we thought was best, and ultimately we agreed that we had saved the best till last. Liam Pickering and his younger associate, James Pitcher, were the best candidates for the job.

I had received a couple of enquiries from the other management companies following our meetings, wishing me Merry Christmas and gently probing to see if I had reached a decision. Finally, it reached the point where I needed to let them know. Dad was adamant that I had to 'do the right thing', by which he meant calling each of the agents I had met with to tell them I would be going with someone else.

This was a horrifying prospect to me. I had never given someone bad news like this before, and I hated letting people down. 'Can't I just text them?' I asked.

Dad was firm. 'This is part of being an adult,' he told me.

Towards the end of January, we set off on a drive together with four phone calls to make: three bad ones, one good one. We drove towards Bells Beach, and I used the Bluetooth in the car to call the first three in turn and tell them that I wasn't going to sign with them. Two of them took it well— they appreciated my courtesy and respected my decision.

The third call was different. 'Well, that's really disappointing, Tom,' came the angry reply. He wanted to know who I was signing with, and I informed him of my choice. 'Really? Are you sure? They've got a lot of high-profile players. You won't get any attention. I think you're making a mistake.'

A rush of guilt and embarrassment came over me. *Why is this guy having a go at me? Am I not doing the right thing? Why is he mad at me?* I tried to justify my decision to him at first, but then I summoned the courage to say, 'Look, there's nothing you can say that's going to change my mind.'

The conversation ended abruptly after that, and shame washed over me. I had liked everyone that I had met with, and I hated upsetting them. It was all really confronting for me, but Dad was well versed in having difficult conversations at work, and he wasn't pleased. 'Why would he do that? Does he think he's gonna change your mind?' he said, along with a few other annoyed comments. I didn't feel any better.

Dad sensed the way the conversation had affected me, and he tried to help me understand the situation better. 'Look, did you do anything wrong?' he asked.

'No,' I replied.

'Did you conduct the process properly and interview each of these people to see if they were the right fit?' he said.

I nodded.

'Did you do the right thing and call each of them yourself and stand behind your decision?'

I agreed that I had.

'Then you've got nothing to worry about,' Dad insisted. 'In fact, if this is how they react to getting a no, then they've just demonstrated that they weren't the right person for the job anyway. You made the right decision.'

What he said made sense and my discomfort began to ease, although my bitter feeling of having let someone down took some time to fade.

•

January passed, and I was back in classes, training and the business of being in Melbourne. At the end of Year 11, with my future in football seemingly on track, my parents and I had met with the school to discuss me dropping a subject, to help me balance the demands of football and schoolwork in the year ahead.

One subject less would give me four periods a week during normal school hours to complete my homework and prepare for my SACs and exams, creating a much better chance for me to get ahead with my work instead of constantly scrambling to finish things at the last minute. I don't know how I would have managed otherwise, as football was only getting more intense.

I had a footy trip to Europe in first term with the Australian Institute of Sport, the National Carnival at midyear, a full season with the Eastern Ranges, and the AFL Draft Combine and the National Draft looming at the end of the season. It seemed impossible to complete the usual amount of coursework on top of that.

Mum and Dad understood—we agreed that doing four subjects well was better than doing five subjects poorly—but they were also very clear that my education was still a priority. 'We are taking a big leap of faith that you're going to do this the right way,' Mum told me. It was an opportunity for me to succeed, not to slack off.

Mr Mifsud, the Year 12 coordinator and one of my favourite teachers, agreed that the best scenario was for me to do four subjects in Year 12. I had already completed Year 12 Biology, so I would finish the year just one subject shy of the standard six. My school, Luther College, trusted me to do the right thing and the teachers were supportive of my sporting endeavours. It felt nice to be treated like a grown-up. As an added bonus, I got to drop Chemistry, which was the bane of my existence.

•

Going back to school was such an exciting prospect. It meant the football season was approaching, which was thrilling enough, but I felt like I had waited my whole life for that final year to begin. Students came to school with driver's licences, and everyone was suddenly very focused on the future. The first round of SACs was met with a mixture of fear and excitement, and we pored over each other's results, trying to see how we were faring against our peers. Everyone was thinking about what was coming next.

The amount of homework ramped up quickly, and I immediately felt grateful for those extra study periods. I spent my time in the Year 12 study centre, completing as much work as I could, trying my hardest to make homework outside of school hours optional, although that didn't always happen.

I relished in my newfound independence and found school more enjoyable than ever before. We were treated like adults! My teachers respected me and gave me incredible support. I had an amazing group of friends, who were as smart or smarter than me and drove me to do well academically. My friends and I often discussed where we were headed. Many of them were considering a commerce degree, or accounting, and heading towards the 'Big Four' accounting firms.

I had no interest in that world, but I knew that I wanted to continue studying. My parents had always said, 'School comes first'—in fact, they repeated it so often it would ring in my head, and it was certainly at the front of my mind when I was planning my future. I wanted to attend university in 2014 regardless of whether I was drafted or not.

I was eyeing a degree in electrical engineering. It was Dad's field, and I was interested in doing something that he could guide me with in the long-term. So electrical engineering seemed like a good option, although I sensed that it would be challenging with so much maths involved. Nevertheless, I began researching course options as the year progressed and realised that a tertiary entrance ranking score of 92 would get me into courses in both Melbourne and Sydney, depending on where I was drafted. That gave me something to strive for.

Even with an AFL career on the horizon, I didn't wish Year 12 away. I could sense the complexity of my life increasing, and I wanted to enjoy the end of my school life. It felt all year like we were on the verge of something big, a new chapter in our lives. We talked about it all the time.

'I can't wait to finish school!'

'Do you think we will be close next year?'

'I hope so.'

'Of course we will!'

I knew my life was going to change completely the moment I left school—that I would leave many of my friends behind as they went off to university and I went off to preseason training somewhere, trading my classmates for teammates.

But I was also planning for the longer term, considering what my career would be after football. I knew my footy career could be short-lived, because this was something they drilled into us at state level and in the TAC Cup. 'The average AFL career is only three and a half years!' I heard it on repeat.

So while that year was increasingly filled with noise and excitement around my football prospects, so loud that it permeated my school and social life, I escaped by working hard on my education. Homework became the perfect excuse for me to put my headphones in, put my head down and drown out the attention that was starting to bombard me.

'How did you go last weekend?'

'How many goals did you kick?'

'How many touches did you have?'

'Who are you playing this weekend?'

'What number in the draft will you go?'

'Have any clubs spoken to you?'

These questions were distracting, and some of them were impossible to answer. If you gave too much information about how you'd been playing, it sounded like you were counting your disposals; too little, and you sounded arrogant or dismissive. I struggled to work out what the 'right' thing to say was. It was never simple. Playful ribbing from my close friends was great—we did it to each other and it kept me feeling normal—but the constant discussions about me, especially in front of me, made me feel like the centre of attention all the time. It became exhausting, and it only intensified as the year progressed towards the National Draft.

When the bell rang at the end of a school day, I didn't feel the sense of relief that my classmates did. I felt like I was transitioning from one part of my life to another. It wasn't a bad feeling—in fact, I loved the way that both my schooling and my football stimulated me, and with my schoolwork under control, I felt free to dive into my training unimpeded by thoughts of SACs or assignments. Changing out of my stiff, sweaty school uniform and into my footy gear was a liberating moment I had at least three days a week.

I was elated every time I walked into the change rooms in Kilsyth, keen to catch up with my other group of friends, who came from all over the eastern region of Melbourne. Almost everyone I went to school with at Luther College came from similar backgrounds: we were the kids of hard-working tradespeople and professionals. I loved the diversity at Eastern, where my friends included other private school kids but also kids from the local high school, and a few who had already finished school and were in the workforce. It didn't matter where anyone came from when we were playing football together.

•

Back in January that year, when I arrived at Kilsyth for the first day of preseason training at the Eastern Ranges, I immediately felt a sense of occasion. There was something serious about the room and the way the players were moving.

In 2012, we had been an underwhelming, disappointing and irrelevant side on the bottom of the ladder. With that came an undeniable lack of expectations and consequences.

We didn't matter to the teams we played, and we didn't have anything to aspire to, other than simple pride in our performance. This year it would be different. No more excuses, no more waiting around. We had high expectations of ourselves and the team, and it was clear from day one that our coaches felt the same.

'This is a big year for the club and for many of you,' Darren Bewick told us. He was Eastern's head coach, known to us as 'Boris'. 'But we have a lot of work to do.'

I was in good condition and had filled out a little over the previous twelve months, no longer the skinny sixteen-year-old I had been the year before. I was stronger, more confident overhead and in one-on-ones, and felt the best physically that I ever had. The team was stronger too. Unlike the year before, where the line-up changed from week to week, this season we had a core group of players who were driving the training standards and pushing the team forward. We reached the end of summer training with great optimism, but still we had no idea where we sat against the other teams. Anything could happen.

I was terribly nervous before our opening game, against Oakleigh. I could feel the weight of expectations surrounding me, doubling the pressure I had placed on myself. We played well: we had clearly improved from the year before, and I contributed strongly with four goals. Yet I felt empty afterwards—more than empty, I was practically disappointed.

It was strange for me to be a part of a team that played well and won, rather than being a shining light in a losing season. I wasn't recognised in the best players of the match, so instead of celebrating the win, I was consumed by my own performance. *I've got to be better. Why did I miss that shot? How did I drop that mark?* Every little mistake haunted me in the days after the game; I couldn't stop thinking about it. I didn't play at Eastern the following week, and I was disappointed that I'd missed the opportunity to begin the season with a bang.

The following week, I played for the Australian Institute of Sport (AIS) squad at the MCG. We played against Collingwood's VFL side, and I performed well, taking ten marks and kicking a goal in a heavy loss. More importantly, I had performed well against 'men', answering a constant question about whether my success in junior football was attributable simply to me being a 'man child'.

The AIS squad was the best of the best young players in the country, those deemed most likely to be drafted that year. It was the place to be if you wanted to get onto an AFL list. The squad had access to resources that other young footballers could only dream of—expert coaches and training programs, training camps and exposure to AFL clubs—but the ultimate purpose was a series of showcase matches in Europe as part of a national team. I felt fortunate to be selected, but of course it only complicated my schedule. It was just week two of the football season and already I had started the back and forth between teams that would dominate my year.

I had to be flexible with my training and games schedule. Some weeks I would train all week at Eastern before playing elsewhere on the weekend; other weeks I wouldn't train at Eastern at all but would turn up on game day. And there were a variety of combinations in between.

I began to hate the sense of ceremony that greeted me when I returned to Eastern from playing at the AIS or with Vic Metro. I hated being treated differently or being the centre of attention—I just wanted to be part of my team, and leave the uncomfortable world of representative football behind me. A small voice in my head told me one thing, over and over: *Don't be arrogant. Don't be big-headed.* It felt like everyone was waiting for me to act differently because of my success.

I came to understand an unfortunate reality that comes with junior players like me who had all of these opportunities: my movement from week to week was disruptive to the team. As I moved in and out of the side, I was often taking players' spots who had played well the week before, and who would have been selected again if I wasn't there. It made me so uncomfortable, and I hated feeling that way. I was trying my best, but I was caught playing for three teams at once, and the strange balance was driving me crazy. I just wanted to play footy.

Meanwhile, I began to get odd looks walking down the street. People would wave at me and say hello. Complete strangers stopped me for a chat at games, or yelled out my name across the oval—and not just at my home grounds or my local club, but at representative games. It started to feel like a target was plastered on my back, as if people couldn't miss me. They all wanted something from me but I didn't understand what.

I did my best to apply Mum's mantra to every inter-action—'Mind your manners,' she always said—but it was difficult. These people knew me, but I didn't know them. I was walking blindly into conversations with people who were prepared, who had things they wanted to say to me, while I just nodded awkwardly. *How do they even know who I am? What was the point of that conversation? Why are they being so nice to me?*

I enjoyed the attention at first, but soon it just became uncomfortable to be in public. It took up time and energy which I preferred to spend on the people who really knew me, not the ones who barely did. I started wearing caps and hoodies wherever I went, especially at games, and prepared responses to the common questions—although really, for me, there was no easy answer.

•

The media coverage of my burgeoning career really ramped up that season, ahead of the 2013 National Draft. I was written about in the local papers, on blogs and on football forums, and I was often sent, shown or read the opinions of others. The coverage wasn't all positive. It was a weird mix of people singing my praises and trying to poke holes in the story of my success, which always rang louder in my head. I didn't know how to ignore it. I took every criticism personally.

In the middle of the season, Eastern played against the Bendigo Pioneers at Box Hill City Oval, winning by 54 points. I kicked three goals and five behinds—it was one of those 'almost' games, where I was just a goal or a handball away from really dominating. After the game, I watched my direct opponent being named best on ground, and it stung. *Had I played that poorly?* I couldn't comprehend how I had been overlooked.

I complained to Dad about it during the week, but he didn't give me the answer I wanted. 'Well, he did some good things, and you didn't play your best game,' he told me.

'So if I play full-back and my opponent has eight shots on goal, that's a win?' I whined.

'They are measuring him against you,' Dad said.

I couldn't swallow my pride. What made matters worse was that in reviewing the game, I saw that I had made errors, and I could have been better. I had missed goals I would normally have kicked, I had given away free kicks, and I'd had moments of selfishness that didn't look good at all. Boris let me know in no uncertain terms that the last of these, in particular, was unacceptable.

Still frustrated, I spoke to my forwards coach, Luke McCormack, who was more understanding than Boris. 'You kick the goal, no one questions it,' he told me. 'You miss, everyone does.'

He was right, but I wasn't ready to hear that either. People wanted me to be a standout player but then criticised me for trying to stand out. I felt like I was being held to a different standard than everybody else. *It's not fair*, I thought. That week left a bitter taste in my mouth.

•

I found solace that week, and every week after, in my schoolwork. I had always loved leaving school to go to football, but now I was beginning to find comfort in being 'normal', and being treated like everyone else at school. The number of goals I had kicked on the weekend was completely irrelevant when I sat down for a Maths Methods test or hit the downball courts. My friends were interested in how I was going, but they knew enough about me already so they didn't need to impose. They didn't hero-worship me—they treated me like a friend. If they wanted to know something about my football, they would ask and I would answer, and we would both move on with our days. I liked the simplicity of that.

Still, I loved being good at football. I was proud of it, and excited about my future, but it was fast becoming clear to me that I didn't like or want the attention that came with it—particularly not the critical or negative parts. To avoid the bad stuff, I would immerse myself in my studies, then I'd go and play the best football possible, and then I'd return to school and try to blend in again as much as possible. School was just as time-consuming as footy that year, if not more so, but at school I was treated like a person.

I felt like I was living two lives—one part football, one part school—with my family and friends floating somewhere in between. Not even they could avoid the growing interest in my football career, though, as the conversation at family gatherings, birthdays and other occasions frequently turned towards the subject. In these settings, where I had once felt so normal, I was now starting to feel out of place.

At Norwood games, Dad would wander over to the clubrooms at half time to get a couple of beers and say hello to his mates, leaving me alone for a bit. I preferred watching the game alone, undistracted and undisturbed, than dealing with the barrage of questions I knew I'd get on the other side of the oval. Unfortunately, this meant Dad had to explain why I was avoiding everyone, but we had agreed it was best. 'You'll never get left alone over there,' he said. I sensed that the attention made Dad uncomfortable too. If they couldn't talk to me, they were happy to talk to him about me.

At seventeen years old I was 198 centimetres and 105 kilograms, and I couldn't blend in anywhere. It was my biggest advantage on the sporting field, but the biggest challenge I had to contend with when I was off it. I loved being tall, but I hated being told, 'Wow, you're tall!' by every single person I met. Like I hadn't noticed. With my height and my growing fame as a footballer, it was impossible for me to fly under the radar. But the weight of a thousand conversations with strangers dragged me down, so I did my best to avoid them.

•

I had a level of certainty and confidence heading into the Vic Metro selections in 2013. The year before, my mind had been clouded with worry and nerves about my performance, my *worthiness*. I found it crippling to feel on the outer all the time, but now things were different. I was the AIS squad player, the leading goalkicker from the 2012 season, the most talked about key forward in the country. It felt like 2013 was my year. I didn't need luck— I was ready.

This certainty didn't make me complacent or lazy; instead, it give me a refined sense of focus, an expectation of excellence that I placed on myself that didn't leave any room for fear, anxiety or doubt, just the knowledge that it was my time.

I wouldn't have to repeat the dismal trip north to Darwin that I had made the year before; this year the first game was in Queensland, but those of us who were in the AIS squad or in good form were not required to play.

In the lead-up, we had to select a leadership group, and I wanted to be a part of it. I even wondered if they'd make me captain. The night we were due to find out, Anton Grbac pulled me aside at training. 'Tommy, I want you to know that we have decided we are going with Luke McDonald as captain this year,' he told me. 'It's not because we don't think you're capable, we just think that Luke is in a better position, especially being a father-son selection. You have enough on your plate.'

I didn't feel anything about this, particularly. Their decision made sense, and I was actually relieved not to add the burden of captaincy to my plate. I trusted Anton—he had proven time and time again that he had my best interests at heart. I didn't have to worry about anything other than my training standards, my performance and the way I treated those around me. I could lead by example on the football field, without the burden of the ceremonial component of the role. I relished the idea of playing in our second game, against NSW/ACT the following week.

The squad returned from Queensland with that all too familiar sense of disparity between some players and others. Some walked in proudly, happy with their performances; others skulked in with their tails between their legs, undoubtedly thinking the same thing I had thought a year earlier: *Have I messed this up completely?*

But not me. I was fresh after a week off, eager to train, eager to be a part of my first state game of the year and my last season representing Victoria.

We were to play at Princes Park that weekend, against the weaker Division Two side from New South Wales and the ACT, and I couldn't bottle up my excitement. I loved playing at Princes Park. I was comfortable with the ground, I knew the tricky pockets of wind and the way the ball flowed. I knew where on the ground I was most comfortable kicking goals and the areas that were more difficult.

I started the game well: the ball felt sticky and clear, I was kicking straight, and by the third quarter I had six goals to my name. I was feeling good. Towards the end of the third quarter, though, I received a vicious knock to my calf, sending pain through the back of my knee. I came from the ground to get it assessed by the physio, intently aware that we were due to play against Western Australia in Perth the following weekend. This game was all but won, so I took no further part, hoping to give myself the best chance of playing in Perth.

I was stiff and sore as the week began, but by Wednesday my calf loosened and I started to feel ready. I trained hard on Thursday to boost my confidence in preparation for the game ahead.

The tone shifted in the lead-up to our game against Western Australia. The coaches looked to sharpen our focus: 'Those first games were to prepare you,' they told us. 'The next three games are the ones that count.' We watched vision of our opponents, holding meetings and talking tactics. It was a dress rehearsal for an AFL match. 'This is as close as it gets,' we were told.

I had one-on-one meetings with the forwards coach, Brent Thiele, to strategise around my individual perfor-mance. We got along so well. He had previously coached the backline and was eager to explore the possibilities of coaching the forwards. I had got to know him well over the past couple of seasons with Vic Metro, and I trusted his judgement. We watched highlights of my likely opponent for the game, Aliir Aliir, who had played particularly well in the first games of the carnival.

Brent emphasised how well Aliir had been playing. 'He's strong, he's fast and he has a great leap,' he said. 'You're not going to be able to just wrestle with him—you will need to use all your tricks.'

I was almost offended. *How good is this guy, really? Has Brent been watching me play? I'll show him.* I prepared mentally and physically, as well as I could, for the biggest challenge of my career to date.

When we walked into the Subiaco stadium the day before the game, my mouth was watering. I saw vast expanses of perfectly manicured grass in long, alternating lines that all seemed to point directly at the goals. It was a dream come true—I couldn't keep the smile off my face. I felt like I belonged, and I couldn't wait for the game.

The following day, game day, the feeling was just as intense, if not more so. The weather was perfect—warm but not hot, with barely any wind and not a drop of moisture. They were perfect conditions for me.

The siren sounded, the game began and before long I had hauled in my first mark, directly opposed to Aliir, which gave me a huge confidence boost. I went back and nailed the set shot. Not long after, I marked again and landed another goal. Then another mark and another goal, and my opponent was changed. I was having one of those days.

A high ball approached the forward 50. I flew and the ball stuck in my hands like glue—perfection. Then I landed. *Crunch.* I had landed horribly on my ankle and a wave of pain surged through my leg, and a wave of uneasiness right behind it.

I doubled over, clutching my ankle in agony, stood up and tried to walk, but my ankle gave way. I bent over again, one hand on my ankle, holding it in place, the other hand holding the ball. I looked up at the clock. It was still the first quarter. We had barely played eleven minutes and I would be lining up for my fourth goal.

I wanted to take my kick but the pain was crippling. I couldn't kick—I couldn't even walk. I had to lie down. This couldn't be happening. The doctors were already scrambling to assist me while the coaches were screaming, 'Make sure Salem kicks it!'

Cristian Salem took the ball from me as I limped off the

ground, supported by doctors and physios. Salem lined it up, nailed it. As my teammates celebrated, I collapsed on the bench, struggling to breathe through the pain.

The team doctor looked over the injury. He gently manipulated my ankle left and right, asking questions, trying to ascertain the damage. He pulled my foot down and towards my other leg, and with an audible *clunk* my ankle dislocated. It reignited the pain and I screamed out in protest, waving the doctor away and asking for pain relief.

I hobbled to the change rooms. Ice was strapped to my ankle and I was given a pair of crutches. My day was over.

I was terrified. *How bad is it? Is it going to ruin my career?* But Anton's words from the year before came to my mind, cutting through the pain and disappointment. All I could think was: *Don't drop your head.* I limped back to the bench on crutches and asked, 'Is there anything you want me to do?'

Anton shook his head. 'Go and rest up, mate.'

Dejected, I sat in the stands with my leg elevated and watched my team win. I was useless.

•

The flight home was unbearable. I was upgraded to business class to accommodate my injury and was given ice throughout the flight to combat the swelling, but nothing seemed to help. The pain was horrible.

I forced a smile and distracted myself with movies until we arrived back in Melbourne, then smiled until I got home from the airport. Around midnight, I was sitting alone in the bathroom with my ankle in a bucket of ice, when the weight of what had happened hit me like a tonne of bricks. I was tired, more mentally than physically. It had taken so much energy to keep myself connected with people that day, to not shrink back into my own disappointment.

Mum came to check on me a couple of times, unsure what to say. 'Do you need anything?' she asked tentatively. I said no. She gave me a hug and left me alone with my thoughts. I didn't sleep much that night.

The next couple of days were a blur of doctors, MRIs and X-rays. This was all brand new to me, I had never had a significant injury before, let alone one like this with an extended recovery timeline. My lack of sleep and the chaos of the preceding days left me feeling hazy and exhausted. I drifted from appointment to appointment, waiting for answers.

During one MRI, I was so tired that I nodded off, only to be woken by a voice in my head: 'Tom, Tom! Is everything okay? You're moving quite a bit in there.' It was the MRI technician. My ankle had been twitching in my sleep, disrupting the picture quality. I straightened up and lay still, but before long I drifted off again and the voice came back: 'Tom! You're doing it again!' The scan process took an hour and a half, but in the end there were still no answers as to how long I would need to recover. The technicians couldn't say.

Eventually, I arrived at Alphington Sports Medicine to see Vic Metro's team doctor, David Bolzonello. He was in a jovial mood when he showed Mum and me into his office.

'Well, you've done a good job, Tom!' David remarked. My ankle was a mess, he said. 'You have an enormous amount of fluid in your ankle and you've completely ruptured the entire lateral side, and managed to damage the medial side as well!' Things clearly weren't right. 'You've completely ruptured all of your lateral ligaments through here,' David said, tracing the image with a pen.

'So, what does this mean?' Mum asked. We had both resigned ourselves to the likelihood that I would need surgery.

But David explained that the best option was to let my ankle heal naturally. 'You've got time—you're only young,' he said. 'It's better this way than to have surgery at your age.'

I asked how long it would take to heal. It was all I really cared about.

'Well, it's hard to say exactly, but three or four months at least,' David replied.

I had already looked at the schedule and knew how long was left. Four months meant my season was over; three months would give me a chance to play finals, if Eastern Ranges made it. This gave me something to grab on to, mentally.

I had great faith in the Eastern side that year. We had draft hopefuls in Mitch Honeychurch, Dan McStay, Michael Apeness and Ben Cavarra, and a star bottom-ager coming through in Christian Petracca. Beyond that, we had a great team and a great group of coaches in Darren Bewick, Luke McCormack and Mark Fisher—we looked likely to at least make finals. This was a better side than the year before: they didn't need me to win.

So I had a little time up my sleeve, and I could at least try to make it back for those last, critical games.

•

The next couple of weeks were so boring. I was in a boot to support my ankle, completing my studies and watching training from a distance. Rehab was tedious and slow, but that wasn't what really bothered me. I felt like I was irrelevant. I had nothing to offer the coaches or the team. The best I could do was give some small pieces of advice from the sidelines, but even that was hollow. I was attached to three teams—the AIS, Vic Metro and Eastern Ranges— but it was difficult to know where I belonged, where I should do my rehab or who I was supposed to answer to.

I comforted myself with the fact that I was a certainty to be drafted by that stage; all that was left to do was speculate about where I would end up. The ankle injury would be behind me by the end of the year. I would complete my first preseason at AFL level, and no one would be the wiser—or so I told myself. I didn't realise that the ankle injury would be with me forever, needing multiple surgeries over my senior football career.

As the weeks and months rolled by, my boredom only increased. I watched Vic Metro fall agonisingly short of another national championship, losing to Vic Country by three points. *If only I could have played, we would have won*, I thought to myself. I was disconnected from everything I had done for the last ten years. I felt like a spectator, not a player, and it was uncomfortable so I spent more and more time on my schoolwork.

I immersed myself in my studies more than ever, becoming closer with my teachers and classmates than ever before. With the four subjects I was doing, I was in class just over half of the time—the rest of the time I was studying, completing coursework, attempting practice exams and SACs, and trying to improve my academic scores.

I had a great rapport with my English teacher, Mrs Sherwin, with whom I shared a love of literature and writing (much to the dismay of one of my great friends, Rhylie Theos, who spent most of her time in class with me telling me how much of a teacher's pet I was). My other subjects didn't come as easily to me—Physics, Maths Methods and Further Mathematics all required hard work—but I enjoyed the grind of practising exam questions over and over again, improving slowly but surely. Nailing a difficult concept for the first time became extremely satisfying.

Unlike football, for me school was unambiguous: if I put the work in, I got the result. In many ways it was an individual pursuit. I enjoyed having a roadmap to success that was almost completely task-oriented; there was a structure to follow and friends to follow it with. Over the previous two years, football had started to take over my life and I'd had to adjust my school schedule and my social life to accommodate it. But being injured levelled everything out. I had equal parts football, school and family, and was genuinely enjoying the balance.

In the background, the noise surrounding my status as a player was growing louder. There were fantasy drafts, football forums and mainstream news articles talking about my prospects. With no effort on my part, I had gone from being a 'top 10 pick' to a 'potential number 1 pick' to a 'projected number 1 pick'—and then, all of a sudden, I was a dead-set certainty to be selected first overall. This all happened within the space of two months, while I was injured. *How am I getting better on the sidelines?* I wondered.

Previously, the attention made me uncomfortable but I felt like I understood it. I would see commentary about my performances, and if it was positive, I would go out and play on the weekend and prove those comments right. If the commentary was critical, I could go out and play on the weekend and prove them wrong. I had agency. That all changed in the lead-up to the National Draft. I was overwhelmed by fluff pieces about my performances and potential. Friends sent me articles, strangers talked to me about it, and my discomfort went to a whole new level.

'Tom Boyd! Number 1!'

'You're a superstar!'

'AFL, mate!'

'GWS next year?'

People had stopped talking with me and started talking at me.

The illogicality of the situation struck me and I thought about it often. People had drawn conclusions about my form from five or six games early in the season, extrapolating those results across a season. Before long, I was 'the next big thing' and the 'best key forward in a long time'. I was being ranked among or above the players I had looked up to the year before. Somehow, Jon Patton, Joe Daniher and Jesse Hogan hadn't gone up in value over the past twelve months, yet I had, while sitting in a moon boot in the stands.

The media coverage was strikingly devoid of any criticism or fact, too. There was no discussion of my cardio levels, my injury, flaws in my game. Those things were all gone. After becoming injured, I had somehow become the perfect player.

I saw this for what it was, and I had doubts about myself—as well as serious doubts about my ankle—and it made me unsure how to handle the attention that was coming my way. I tried to avoid it and hide with my schoolmates, but I felt obliged to agree to the media requests. I didn't mind being in front of the camera, or being interviewed—I was good at it, and thought it was something I was supposed to do—but the words I said became added to the praise I was receiving. *He's well spoken, articulate, professional.* The myth of me as the perfect player grew.

It was obvious that the expectations of me as a player were out of control. I knew I'd had a brilliant start to the season, so much so that my performances were completely unsustainable. Defenders would have focused on me more, or weather would have slowed me down, or (as happened) an injury would come along. But people wanted to believe after the start of the season that I was the best player to come through the draft in a long time as it was an exciting idea. Really, the timing of my injury meant most of my season was left to the imagination, and that imagination was now running wild in football circles.

The heights I had been elevated to were making me feel dizzy. I could hold the feeling at bay, knowing I was unlikely to play again that season, but the pressure was mounting— and eventually I would have to play again. I got the sense that I needed to dominate every game I played to satisfy people, that I couldn't put a foot wrong and that I was destined to be an immediate success in the AFL. I didn't know how I would be able to live up to the legend they were creating for me.

5

BITTERSWEET

The end of Eastern Ranges' 2013 season was rapidly approaching, and my ankle was frustratingly slow to heal. As the weeks progressed, I found it more and more difficult to separate how I was doing with my rehab from my feelings about how others were going on the field. Even the draft talk about me started to die down; it seemed like people had reached a consensus about it and so had lost interest in the subject.

I had always loved watching games of football, but the longer I spent on the sidelines, the less secure I felt about my own ability. It made me uncomfortable and impatient watching other players perform well and receive praise each week. I missed the weekly build-up, being a part of the planning and preparation, the feeling of anticipation ahead of a game. Now I watched from afar as my teammates prepared together, rode the bumps of poor performances and celebrated the good ones. Occasionally I would talk to them, trying to stay engaged, but it was difficult. I wasn't needed.

As it became clear that Eastern were a certainty for the finals, I began to feel optimistic again. The first week of finals was completely off the cards for me as I would be only ten weeks post-injury, but if we made the preliminary final, I might be a chance to play. If we made the Grand Final, surely.

With that in mind, I began to increase the intensity of my rehab. I had something to aim for, and all I could do was hope the boys would keep winning. Before long I became obsessed with returning to play. It was a compelling way to finish my TAC Cup career, and I relished the prospect of returning to the team late in the year and helping them win the premiership.

We ended the season second on the ladder, giving us a double chance and a genuine run at the cup. A victory in the opening round would grant us the following week off, giving me two solid weeks to prepare for the preliminary final. I was filled with energy. This was the first real good news I'd had in three months, and the first indication of any sort of plan for me in the weeks ahead.

The most frustrating thing over the previous weeks had been the number of times I had been told 'Be patient' or 'Do your rehab' or—the worst possible advice—'Just relax'.

I was champing at the bit to return, but I was being told to 'save myself' for the AFL preseason, and that I had 'bigger fish to fry'. I disagreed: the end of my junior career was rapidly approaching, and with it a sweeping amount of change.

It was likely I'd have to move to another city right after the draft, as the Greater Western Sydney Giants had the first and second pick. People were talking about my selection as a forgone conclusion. But I had been at Eastern Ranges since I was fourteen years old. Over the past four years I had attended games, trainings and meetings, and I had become great friends not just with my teammates but with all the staff and volunteers I'd met. I wanted to finish my junior career with a premiership for the club, to make the most of that amazing period of my life.

•

Sean Murphy, our high performance coach, led a special rehab training session for Mitch Honeychurch and me on the morning of the first final. Every session took us one step closer to returning to the side, and we were eager not to miss any. Mitch had been a great teammate of mine since the beginning of our time at Ranges. We'd played together at Eastern and against each other when he played for Vermont, and we shared a desperation not to end our junior careers on the sidelines.

Eastern played that day against the Dandenong Stingrays, with me and Mitch watching from the stands, and from the opening bounce it was a disaster. We came into quarter time down four goals to one, and at half time we were trailing by eight goals to two. It would take a superhuman effort to return from that margin, and it wasn't to be. We finished the game losing comfortably, 89–56. It wasn't a terrible margin but we were never really in the game.

When the final siren went, a feeling of dread came over me. We had lost our double chance, and it seemed more likely then that our team would fall out of the finals as a result. All the promise of that end of season, and my chance of a return, was on a knife-edge. Mitch and I spoke briefly, sharing our dismay about our chances, before heading down to the field to console our teammates.

The following weekend was more of the same. Mitch and I completed a training session on the morning of the game, in which Eastern faced the Northern Knights. This time there were no second chances, but Mitch and I were powerless to affect the outcome. I had never been so nervous watching a game of football in my life. I felt like my career depended on the results of a game I wasn't playing in.

Ranges took an early lead, but the Knights never lost touch. We were fifteen points up at quarter time, 21 at the main change. Three-quarter time saw us leading 10.10 (70) to the Knights' 5.16 (46)—they had been wasteful in front of goal, which saved us from feeling much scoreboard pressure.

Four goals seemed a decent lead to defend with one quarter to play, but still I didn't dare think about victory.

The last quarter was terrifying to watch: with every offensive push the Knights made, I held my breath; every mistake or missed opportunity our team had was equally nerve-racking. Thankfully, the siren sounded with Eastern ahead, the victors by nineteen points. Our season was still alive.

I hadn't done a single football training session since the injury, but it was preliminary final week and the rulebook on ankle rehabilitation wasn't occupying any of my headspace. I came in full of energy to start the week, eager to push along the training schedule with Murph, convinced that I was ready to return.

Forever the voice of reason, Sean made it clear that there were certain things I needed to be able to do physically before I could rejoin the side. 'You can't go out there and get injured in the first five minutes and leave your teammates hung out to dry,' he told me. That message rang in my head all week.

With each day that passed, I felt more pressure. I spent my days at school thinking about how my ankle felt, testing it, doing extra work on my flexibility and trying to avoid any precarious situations that could strain it. When Thursday came around, school felt like it took forever to end. The only thought occupying my mind was the fitness test I had to take at training that evening.

I had started running again about a month earlier, and had experienced consistent calf and ankle pain. The physio told me that I needed to increase my calf strength and ankle flexibility before it would go away. A great friend and physio, Richard Taylor was also a former AFL footballer, and I trusted his opinion. But no amount of agony, treatment or patience had improved the issues I was having.

Our main focus was rehab sessions designed to increase my flexibility, where multiple times a day I had my ankle hooked up to a strap and would have to flex my joint over and over again. It was excruciating. Richard's opinion was that it wasn't worth risking my ankle to play in the finals, but ultimately he conceded it was my decision.

All week, I felt conflicted. *I'll be right*, I thought, but then I heard Sean's and Richard's voices in my head: 'It's not worth the risk.'

If we win this week, I'll be ready.

Will we win this week?

What if I get injured again?

What will people think of me?

The fitness test provided the answer: I was slow, lethargic, sore and immobile. I could play, but the risk of failure was far too high, and so the decision was made, much to the coaches' dismay. Boris had been keeping a close eye on the test, and when we approached he asked, 'No good?' I shook my head. He quickly turned around and walked inside—he and the team had a job to do that weekend, and I wouldn't be a part of it.

I couldn't play, but we didn't need to tell the opposition

that. I was named on the ground and the football circles began to talk excitedly about my return—exactly as we'd hoped. For the third week in a row, Mitch and I would train before the game on the oval outside of Princes Park, preparing in hope of a win today and a Grand Final berth the following week. I was listed as a late withdrawal, in the hopes of throwing our opposition, the Geelong Falcons, into disarray.

After training with Mitch, I got changed and prepared myself for another agonising round of nerves and worry as I watched the game. In the rooms beforehand, I was pulled aside by Andrew Fisher, who had been my head coach two years earlier and was now an assistant coach for the senior team. 'You know you're going to be able to play next week,' he said. 'Now you've just got to trust your teammates to get us there.'

Suddenly I felt better. It wasn't about me—it was about us, the team, and my teammates needed my support more than ever. Worry and nerves turned to excitement as I took my place in the stands.

The game had a fierce opening. Geelong had finished top of the ladder, losing only three games for the year, with an extraordinary percentage of 150. In the two weeks since losing to Dandenong, a thought had been popping in and out of my mind: *Now we have to play Geelong.* There had been a general sentiment that by finishing second on the ladder, we would have a good chance of making the Grand Final, having two very winnable games before presumably confronting the best team that year in the final game of the year. And anything can happen in a Grand Final.

But we had lost in the first round of the finals, so now we found ourselves crossing paths with the top-ranked team a week earlier than we anticipated. With me on the sidelines, we needed a full-forward to compensate, and we had one in Christian Petracca. I had known Christian for some time before we played together at Eastern Ranges, and had competed with and against him in state and representative basketball over the years. He was a year younger than me, but you could never tell. He possessed a great tenacity for ball sports, was strong and powerful, and had enormous hands. His talents were on full display that day.

Half time found us with a score of 7.10 (52) to Geelong's 5.9 (39). Both teams had their chances but my frustration was blinding me to that. *If only we had kicked that one! How did he miss that?!* I was finding it extraordinarily difficult to watch on in such an important game.

It was Geelong's turn to be wasteful in the third quarter, and both Mitch and I were on the edge of our seats, unsure how to feel or when to speak. We held an eleven-point lead going into the final quarter—and then came the surge. Eastern looked inspired, kicking six goals to two to run away with the victory. Mitch and I grabbed each other in excitement, goal after goal, until the final siren sounded.

'We are going to a Grand Final!' we hollered.

Almost instantly, a wave of doubt rushed into my mind. Unlike Mitch, I hadn't proven that I was fit enough yet. He would be clear in a week, but I was still a maybe. *What if I don't get up to play? What if . . . what if . . .* But my self-absorption was deafened out by the cheers in the change rooms—the hugs, laughs and pure, unadulterated joy. Darren Bewick was beaming from ear to ear. I shook Christian's hand and he smiled back at me with his characteristic cheeky smile. I hugged Dan—I was so proud of him.

Eastern Ranges had not been a successful club in the past. We had often been forgotten in favour of teams that were proclaimed 'football factories', known for their history of getting players drafted. We didn't have that reputation, which made it that much sweeter to see Eastern life members like Alf and Mary Pennington, Ian Gooch and John Bigelow see us lining up for only our second ever premiership.

I had so much on my mind as the following week began, and so much hanging in the balance. We were playing Dandenong again, who had certainly bested us in our previous meeting. *But we had been missing players and it was just an off day*, I thought to myself. Every person in the team was almost certainly doing the same mental gymnastics, trying to prepare for the week ahead.

No matter which way I twisted the storyline from our previous encounter—making concessions for how we had played, and assuming that Dandenong couldn't possibly play that well again—I kept arriving at the same conclusion:

I've got to play. I was incapable of thinking anything else. I had spent so much time and energy at Kilsyth Recreation Reserve over the years, as much as any of my teammates. *I deserve to play! And they need me!* These thoughts were loud and constant, but they were offset by the feeling of despair that took me when I considered going out on the field, unprepared, and getting injured again. Or, worse, failing.

Our training session on the Tuesday night didn't settle the issue. No one wanted to risk the possibility of me getting hurt in the week leading into the Grand Final, so I didn't do much at all. 'You're not going to get any fitter now, Tom,' Shaun remarked. 'Just get yourself right for a fitness test on Thursday.' It took all of my self-control for me to overcome the impatience I was feeling. I had to know if I was playing, one way or the other—the suspense was insufferable.

D-day arrived, Thursday night training. I prepared to be put through my paces and my ankle was strapped within an inch of its life. I could barely move it, but I didn't care. I went through a series of drills to test its capabilities, and to my surprise it felt okay. I could change direction, run and mark, and before long I'd completed a reasonably all-encompassing fitness test.

I met with Mark Fisher and Shaun Murphy afterwards. 'How did it feel?' Murph asked.

'Pretty good, actually,' I replied. 'A little stiff, but I've got good movement and that calf pain feels a lot better.'

Darren Bewick walked over to join the conversation. 'Right to go?' he said.

The abruptness of his question caught me off-guard. Darren was a smart operator, and had undoubtedly been watching me being put through my paces. *He really wants me to play*, I realised. 'Yeah, mate, I'm happy,' I replied. 'I'll play.'

I said it casually, but those two words—*I'll play*—had more weight than I could really comprehend. It was thirteen weeks since my injury. I had barely trained, and would be lining up in the biggest game of my life, but the coaches wanted me out there. They told me that me at 75 per cent was enough, and I believed it.

•

The big day at Docklands stadium arrived with more fanfare than any TAC Cup game I had ever played; it was reminiscent of games at the national championships. Among my teammates, I knew I probably felt most comfortable in that arena as I had played there a number of times before, so I tried to calm the nerves of those around me. 'It's just another game!' I told them. 'Today's our day!' I repeated over and over again.

Running out to warm up felt strange. It had been so long since I had been a part of this pre-game ritual. A wall of fatigue hit me almost instantly, and I began puffing and wheezing within the first few minutes. *Oh no.* I wasn't fit enough. A rush of doubt overcame me, cutting through the fatigue. *Am I going to be okay? What can I do?*

I felt trapped but it was too late. I had declared myself fit and I couldn't pull out now—there was no way. Instead, I conserved my energy, trying to hide my fatigue and ensuring I didn't tire myself out too much before the game had even started. There was nothing left to do now but play.

•

The opening quarter was better than I could have hoped for. My instructions were to play close to goal to conserve my energy, and I did exactly that. Relishing the fact that I was always in scoring distance, I kicked three opening-quarter goals, making us quarter-time leaders 4.2 (26) to Dandenong's wasteful 1.4 (10). I had done my job! I started us off well and we were playing good football.

The second quarter was much of the same. We piled on goal after goal, kicking six straight goals and keeping Dandenong goalless. Half time saw us 49-point leaders, and it seemed unfathomable that Dandenong would close the gap from there. But the nightmarish possibility of choking at the finish line sharpened my focus.

'It's nil all! We start again,' the coaches told us. *Stay motivated*, I told myself.

Our mission was clear: win the second half, win the game. In the event, the second half was an obliteration. We ran away winners in what was almost the perfect game of football. Thirteen individual goalkickers made up our 24 goals and eight behinds, for a total of 152 points. We were 112-point winners, the biggest margin in TAC Cup history. I finished with four goals, the most important of which had come in the first quarter. I had contested well, but had missed marks and made mistakes through fatigue. It wasn't my best performance, but it was enough—and anyway, it wasn't about me.

The moments following the game were bittersweet. The sweetness was in the smiles on everyone's faces, the hugs we exchanged with friends, parents, coaches and teammates. We had done it. Champions! Premiers! But I also felt a quiet sadness as I walked around the Docklands stadium afterwards. It was all over. My time as a junior was done—it had finished in the best way possible, but it was over.

I was so happy for everyone, and proud of what we had achieved. It felt like the day was four years in the making, ever since Ben Cavarra (who was best on ground in the Grand Final), Mitch Honeychurch and I had first walked into Eastern Ranges together. We hadn't known what was ahead as fourteen-year-olds—we just wanted to play. It had been such a wonderful time. I was excited for what was to come, but I knew that I would miss this part of my life.

•

With our season behind us, and with Hawthorn crowned as the 2013 AFL premiers, the footballing world looked to the future. With that came an added layer of attention on the National Draft.

The Draft Combine is a series of athletic trials held at both national and state level. Throughout the event, players are put through an array of tests designed to assess their form and talent. Some of the testing is just your physical measurements (height, weight, skinfolds) and some is skills-based, such as your kicking and handballing. Other trials look at your speed and aerobic capacity, and some test your reaction times. Overall, the combine is designed to place the young best players around the country in a fishbowl, measuring their skills in all areas in such a way that they can be scrutinised and ranked.

Every club attends the Draft Combine, and they are all moving players up and down their own draft board, based on their interpretation of the testing data and on interviews they hold with the players. For a player to be invited, a number of AFL clubs need to nominate you as a player of interest, so being invited to the national Draft Combine is a fairly good indication that you will be selected in the draft. Those who don't get quite enough interest are invited to take part in smaller, state-based combines, which generally means they're in the mix for the later rounds of the draft.

Unlike some of my teammates, I didn't feel a huge amount of anticipation leading into the combine. I had my performances on the field to lean on, and they were the most important thing . . . *Right?* I became less sure of myself as the combine got closer. With only a month between our premiership and the trials, I had no time to get fit, and no time to change much about how I felt or looked.

I became increasingly nervous about my weight and skinfolds. I had heard first-hand descriptions of the grilling players had endured when being interviewed by AFL clubs; some were genuinely frightening. Certain clubs were notoriously tough in their interviews. I knew that my on-field performances were undeniable, but I was terrified that my running capacity or fat levels would be used as ammunition against me. The thought of coming under fire made me queasy.

The feelings I had about my fitness levels were only trumped by the concerns I had about my ankle injury. I had managed to play in the Grand Final, yes, but since then I had struggled to improve my running times, I was always sore and I struggled to complete some of my training sessions. The idea of finishing a three-kilometre time trial was unfathomable.

I opened up to Shaun Murphy about my concerns, and later to the support staff at the AIS. We agreed on a couple of things. Firstly, that I shouldn't have played in the TAC Cup Grand Final; really, I was in no condition to play a game of football, and in any other circumstances I wouldn't have played.

Secondly, we agreed that it would be irresponsible for me to complete the rigorous athletic testing of the Draft Combine with my ankle in the condition it was. There was a high chance that I would re-injure it, and that made no sense, given my expected standing in the draft.

I breathed a sigh of relief. One possibility of embarrassment was off the table; now I had to worry about the skinfold testing. I started planning: when I would eat, what I would eat and when I would consume water.

Murph suggested doing a skinfold test at Eastern Ranges ahead of the Draft Combine to see where I was at. I dodged it for as long as I could, but finally ran out of excuses. Standing there in the gym at Kilsyth Reserve, adding up the numbers in my head, I knew it was not looking good. I began to sweat. I scored somewhere in the 70s and felt a wash of shame and despair. *How will I get through the combine? Everyone will know.*

I was at a loss. This chink in my armour affected me more than anything. It was just one small thing, but it felt like it would spoil my entire reputation. I cast my mind back to all the things I had eaten that weren't 'healthy' over the last few months, and felt a wave of regret and frustration with myself. *Why did you do that? Why did you eat that? You're such an idiot.*

There was only one thing I could do. *If I'm light, it won't be so bad*, I told myself. I decided to skip meals before the testing started. I didn't need the energy to train. I tried not to drink much water either. I controlled the only things I could.

The national Draft Combine was held at Docklands in early October 2013. The day began with introductions and formalities, and then the testing got underway, beginning with measurements. It felt like I was waiting for ages before my name was called, but finally I was put out of my misery and the moment of truth arrived.

I measured in at 200 centimetres tall—a small consolation prize. I had never quite got over the 199-centimetre mark previously, though I'd tried! My weight was as low as I could have hoped for, around 102 kilograms. *Thank God*, I thought. *Now I can eat something.* All I had left was my skinfolds.

Unlike with Shaun, the skinfold tests were being done rapidly, as there were so many players to get through. Fat was pinched, scores read out, a cumulative score created, and the next person was up. I held my breath when my turn came. 'Sixty-one,' the assessor barked, and I was through.

I couldn't believe it—it simply wasn't possible that my reading had changed so quickly. It was obviously down to the speed of the process, but I had never felt so relieved. The worst of the combine was well and truly behind me.

I spent most of the next couple of days at Docklands watching the combine from the stands, excused from the athletics because of my injury. I chatted with recruiters who were watching on, and a few journalists. I spoke to Cal Twomey, an AFL reporter with whom I had grown friendly during the AIS trip to Europe earlier that year, but mostly I was pretty bored.

When the trials were done, the draftees waited to receive schedules for their club interviews, the next big hurdle we had to overcome. To my disappointment, my schedule was basically empty. It wasn't really surprising, as many clubs considered me a certainty to be taken at pick 1, and therefore out of their grasp, but I didn't enjoy being left out. I was asked to speak with the GWS Giants, the Western Bulldogs and Melbourne. My excess of spare time was obvious to others as well as me, and probably out of pity West Coast offered to interview me too.

Media outlets interviewed me about the upcoming draft, and I chatted with staff I knew at the combine to fill in the time. I quite enjoyed talking to the journalists I met. They were friendly people, interested in what made me tick. I prepared myself as best I could for the interviews, telling myself I had nothing to fear. *After all, what's the worst they can say?* I always loved talking to new, interesting people, and the constant refrain of, 'Wow, you speak really well!' always made me proud.

My first meeting was in a corporate suite at Docklands with the Western Bulldogs. I was relatively comfortable on the way in, but I stepped through the door and found the room packed with people. There must have been fifteen staff from the club there.

'Hi, Tom,' said Jason McCartney, the list manager, and he

went around the room introducing the recruiting staff and their list management team. I was surprised that even the senior coach, Brendan McCartney, was there. I felt unnerved by the crowd that greeted me, and I wasn't sure who to look at when answering questions. *Who are the most important people here?* I wondered. But the conversation flowed freely, and I felt more and more comfortable as it went on.

By the end of the meeting, it was clear to me that the Bulldogs had a serious desire to draft me, however they only had pick 4, so it was likely they would be too low to get a chance—at least if the consensus about my prospects was correct. I left the room feeling good. *That wasn't so bad.* In fact, I felt better than good—I'd loved talking to these high-level professionals about my career, and I enjoyed being able to keep pace with them.

Next up was the Greater Western Sydney Giants, and I was interested to see how the conversation would play out. The meeting was nowhere near as full—only six or seven people from the club were there, one of whom was their coach, Leon Cameron. Unlike the conversation with the Bulldogs, where their coach had sat at the back of the room, only contributing to the conversation a couple of times, Leon led this conversation. He made a strong first impression on me. He was clearly intelligent, with a gravity to him. He commanded attention, like a good coach should, and was distinctly different to most other people I had spoken to that week.

'Tom, we're going to be straight with you,' he began. 'We are going to take you at number one.'

Leon's bluntness surprised me, but I appreciated having this confirmed, and not having to guess anymore. I had spoken to the club earlier but this was straight from the horse's mouth. Oddly, I wasn't sure how to respond. I didn't know how to feel. It was the single biggest piece of information I had ever received in my life. 'Thanks,' I mustered eventually.

Leon continued: 'Now, you obviously can't tell anyone this, except your family of course. Everyone else will need to find out on draft night.'

I nodded—*of course.*

Leon began to describe the club, where they had been, what they were working on and what they were striving for in the future. Unlike my first interview, this was less of a pitch and more of an information session. I was finding out what was going to happen next.

After we said our goodbyes, reality set in. I was going to be the first pick in the AFL National Draft. Number 1! It was the stuff of legend, happening to me—mind-boggling! But I couldn't tell anyone. It was an open secret really, but I still couldn't say it out loud.

I found a quiet corner in the grandstand where no one was in earshot and called Dad.

'How's the day going?' he asked.

We hadn't seen each other for a couple of days as I was staying in the city.

'Not bad,' I replied, barely able to contain myself, eager to get past the small talk. Midway through his next question, I blurted out: 'I met with the Giants and they are going to take me at pick one!' Now that I'd said it out loud for the first time, suddenly it was real.

'Well done, mate, that's good,' Dad said calmly. It wasn't the time to celebrate. 'What else did they say?'

I went on to describe the meeting and those who had been there, but all the finer details seemed insignificant compared to the news I had already delivered.

Soon enough, I had to get off the phone. I had my final scheduled meeting, with Melbourne, to attend. The strangeness of it hit me as I walked around to the meeting room Melbourne had been assigned. *Do I need to be here? What are they going to say?* I was attending a job interview for a job I didn't need, because I already had a job at another company. Draftees don't get to choose where they go.

I had no idea how the meeting was going to go, so I gathered myself up, took a deep breath and knocked on the door. There were ten or so staff from Melbourne in the room, and the seriousness and tension was obvious. I had met with their recruiting staff previously, during my time with the AIS, but there were many strangers in the room as well. One stood out: legendary coach Paul Roos was standing against the wall at the back of the room. His presence surprised me—I found him mildly terrifying.

The interview got underway, and it was more formal than the earlier ones. They pressed me harder on my answers, and showed less emotion and encouragement when I responded. It began to feel more like an interrogation than an interview. I felt uncomfortable, but continued to answer the questions well. Many I had heard before and was ready for; some were new, but I thought carefully and answered accordingly.

After fifteen minutes or so of that, Paul entered the conversation. 'What is your biggest weakness?' he asked.

I responded in the way I had previously: 'I'm continuing to work on my aerobic fitness—I think that's the biggest part of my game I'd like to improve on.'

Paul held a document up and read from it. 'Let me see here. Three-kilometre time trial, 12:39. Whoa! That's bad. Really not good enough.' He shook his head.

A horrible feeling surged through my gut. I knew it wasn't a good time, but I'd only had one attempt, on a hot day in Canberra at the beginning of preseason. Blushing, I acknowledged what he said, but noted that my time would have improved significantly since then.

'How are you supposed to compete at the top level with that running ability?' Paul responded. 'Kurt Tippett is the same size as you and he runs a much better time.'

I was shocked. No one had ever pushed me this hard on my flaws. I did not like it. I stumbled over a disjointed version of what I had said earlier—there was really nothing more I could say. Paul clearly wasn't satisfied with the answer I had given, so we moved on and the interview ended, awkwardly.

I was furious. *What are AFL preseasons for, if not to get fitter? What is his problem? Kurt Tippett? The guy has done eight years of AFL, of course he's fitter than me!* And then: *Who cares, they aren't going to pick me anyway.* We had spent very little time in the meeting discussing what I was good at. Instead, the coach had focused on the one glaring weakness in my game. I wondered if they had targeted me for a reason.

Later that day, I called my friend Nick Vlastuin, who had had a wildly successful first season with Richmond after being drafted at pick 9 in 2012.

'How's the combine going?' he asked. 'Any clubs grilled ya?'

He was eager to hear the gossip, and I told him about my experience with Melbourne.

He laughed. 'Mate, don't worry about it—they absolutely grilled me last year! Kept saying that other players in the draft were far better than me. It was pretty rough.'

I was shocked to hear this. *It wasn't about me?*

'They just put you under the pump to see how you respond. I wouldn't worry about it,' Nick said.

Suddenly, all I could think of was what I should have said, and how I should have stood up for myself more. If it was a test of my mental resilience, I'm not sure how well I fared. But I felt slightly better. It wasn't personal—it was a tactic they had clearly used for some time. Still, they had picked the right spot to push me on, and some residual bitterness remained.

•

With the Draft Combine behind me, football took a back seat. My Year 12 exams were looming, and with only a few weeks left to prepare, I dived into my studies. This was a really significant time for me. My parents had made a lot of concessions along the way to ensure I could follow my footballing path, but they had never compromised on my education. I was determined to do well.

I had been underprepared for my exams in Year 11, and I swore I would not make the same mistake again. I dived into practice exams, essay prompts and catch-ups with my teachers. It was comforting to know that I was going through the same thing as all of my classmates, which helped to drown out the noise and media speculation around the draft. I had prepared for thirteen years to finish high school, and I wanted to do it well.

I continued to go to football training but it became a minor part of my routine, a way to break up the monotony of another practice essay or calculus question. After a while, the repetition of going over the same problems again and again became unbearable, so I turned my focus to the subjects whose teachers I felt the most engaged with. *My bottom two subjects won't count as much*, I thought—until I realised that with only five subjects in total, I needed great results in at least four of them to get the ATAR score I had hoped for.

After countless hours trying to grasp the concept of vectors of force for my upcoming Physics exam, I'd had enough. My teacher, Mr Osborne, was undeniably smart—possibly too smart. The concepts would not stick in my head, and after asking him to explain it again and again, I realised that Physics simply wasn't for me. Each time I'd fail to grasp an idea, Mr Osborne would look slightly more exasperated, though most of my friends in class weren't faring much better. It was as though we had left most of the learning for the last month of the year. It was clear that Physics was going to be my bottom subject.

The first one came around quicker than I anticipated, a gruelling three-hour ordeal in the form of an English exam. It consisted of three essays: one language analysis, one context essay and one book review. This was my best subject by far. I had topped the class in English all year with the help of the brilliant Mrs Sherwin, who I loved. I was proud of my writing and didn't want to let her down. My preparation had been immaculate, each practice essay slightly better than the one before, all scoring 9/10 or 10/10, over and over again. I had toiled through quotes from our focus book, *Ransom* by David Malouf, and read newspaper articles to analyse the persuasive language they used.

It was all going perfectly until the final practice essay I handed in came back marked 7/10, which made me panic.

Walking into the exam, all I could think was, *Don't mess this up now!* I couldn't think of anything worse than stumbling at the finish line.

I went through my reading time and began writing, and before long I was in a great rhythm. By the end of my third essay, I looked up to see that I still had twenty minutes left! I pored over my essays, convinced I had missed something, forgotten something. But I couldn't find anything to change. I was elated when I walked out. *English is done!*

The rest of the exam period continued, a war of attrition. I could feel the energy flagging among my schoolmates. Our attention to detail began to fade, and the exam preparation groups got smaller as people lost the will to study. In stages, my classmates finished their final exams, and were released. My final exam was still looming: the dreaded Physics exam.

I had all but given up by the time I walked in to do it. My brain was completely saturated, with no more room for information, and I just wanted these exams to be over. I'd prepared with as much vigour as I could muster, but I was hoping for an admirable pass at best. It didn't matter. I will never forget how good it felt to walk out of that exam room. It was the most liberating feeling I'd ever had.

•

Some friends came over to my place in Ringwood to enjoy a couple of hard-earned beers. It was a Wednesday afternoon, and most of my classmates had finished their final exams and were eagerly talking about schoolies week and their summer ahead. We laughed and told stories as the afternoon wore on, but I felt a kind of melancholy about the whole scene. I knew it was the last time I could do this with my friends.

The National Draft was a week away. I would be heading to the Gold Coast for the ceremony, a major event in the football calendar, and my life as a professional athlete would begin a few days later. There would be no schoolies and no summer with friends for me. I had already begun packing my bags for the move to Sydney.

The week ahead was daunting. After months of waiting for the draft, the busyness of my exam period had distracted me from the rapidly approaching date. It had felt like the day would never arrive, and now it felt all too close. I had so much to organise and Mum was on my case, knowing full well that if she didn't help me, I would leave it to the last minute to pack. I was finding it difficult. *How do you pack for a trip that doesn't have an end?* I had one advantage, though: at least I knew where I was going.

I had to get my car to Sydney, a champagne gold 2006 Subaru Outback that was being freighted interstate for me. Mum kept lingering around me, asking if I needed help with anything, trying to help me organise things, but Dad steered clear. He was busy with work and didn't have the time (or interest, to be honest) to work out which clothes I needed for a Sydney summer. He was happy for me to figure out how to leave the nest. Mum cried more than a few times. The smallest things would set her off—a conversation or an old photograph. I had never lived away from home before.

The 2013 AFL National Draft was held at the Gold Coast Convention Centre on Thursday, 21 November. At the ceremony that evening, the top 10 draft picks would be announced and presented on stage with their new club's jumper. Fifteen or sixteen players were invited each year to make sure the top 10 were all in attendance, but also to create a bit suspense. Sometimes, a club with a high draft pick would make a surprise selection, throwing the subsequent picks into total carnage as the clubs scrambled to meet their recruitment priorities. With this process came a certain amount of tension. Every player invited to the draft was almost certainly going to be selected, but they didn't yet know which state they would be in the following week, let alone which team they would be playing for.

With the intensity of the media coverage ramping up in the days leading into the draft, I decided it would be a good idea to take my surfboard up to the Gold Coast. I needed a distraction. We were arriving early on the Thursday, and I'd have plenty of hours to kill before we were required at the event. I could feel myself getting nervous, knowing that nothing was final until it was final. *What if the Giants have changed their mind and not told me? Do I need to make a speech? What am I supposed to say?* My mind was running wild.

At the Gold Coast airport, while waiting for my bags to arrive on the carousel, I heard a voice calling my name, 'Tom, Tom!' As I turned around, I saw a TV camera and a man holding a microphone. 'Mark Stevens, Channel Seven,' he said. 'How are you, Tom? Mind if we have a quick chat?' He had caught me completely off-guard.

'Yeah,' I responded, still a bit confused. 'Do you mind if I grab my things first?' I picked up my surfboard from the oversize luggage area and turned around to see my parents looking extremely uncomfortable. It wasn't my first TV interview, but they had never seen anyone approach me so abruptly, and I doubt they were expecting media at the airport.

Mark and I chatted briefly about the night ahead, my feelings leading into the draft and the likelihood of me being taken at pick 1. I played a straight bat and the interview was blandly positive and relatively painless. Mum and Dad seemed relieved as we moved off to grab a hire car and head to our hotel.

•

After we checked in, I realised there was nothing to do but sit around and wait. Twitter and the football news media were raging with speculation about the night ahead, but it didn't do my nerves any good to follow it. It was exhausting and extraordinarily competitive. *Now is a good time for a surf,* I thought.

I went downstairs with my board and towel, wondering if there would be any journalists lying in wait, but there weren't. I managed to get out into the water undisturbed.

I surfed a little and thought a lot. I considered my future, both tonight's event and the weeks to come. *This is the last bit of peace I'm going to get for a while.* I plotted what I was going to say once my selection was announced, and who I was going to thank. It seemed silly not to prepare something.

Before long, my time surfing was up. I had to get myself ready for the night ahead.

•

Sporting my Eastern Ranges polo shirt, dress pants and shoes, I arrived at the Gold Coast Convention Centre. The venue was decked out in black, enormous banners with the images of previous number 1 draft picks hanging from the walls. In front of the stage there were a number of round tables, each set for ten people. We shared ours with Lewis Taylor, a super-talented midfielder from the Geelong Falcons, and his family.

Before long, the media poured in, alongside the recruiters, the list managers, the coaches and some fans as well. Then the proceedings began with some long, introductory speeches. Finally it was time for the draft. My nerves had reached fever pitch by the time it started.

'Selection number 1, GWS Giants,' AFL CEO Andrew Demetriou began.

The recruitment staff from the Giants responded, 'Player Number 214227, Thomas Boyd, Eastern Ranges, Norwood Football Club.'

There it was.

Number 1. Everything felt surreal. I stood up as the room erupted in applause. I hugged my parents. *Wait, is this really happening?* I panicked. *Did they actually read my name out or did I just assume?* I looked around at everyone's faces, checking to see if anyone was looking at me strangely. They weren't. I breathed out, continuing up onto the stage to meet Leon Cameron, shake his hand and smile as he handed me my GWS jumper. *It's really happening.* Leon and I posed for a photo together, then I was ushered to the lectern to meet the MC.

I had waited so long for this moment and had rehearsed it a thousand times in my head. But an overwhelming feeling of strangeness had swept over me as my name was announced, and it took me a moment to compose myself and remember the words I had prepared. I had made a bet with Dad earlier that day that I was going to use the word 'superseded' in my speech, and so I did. When I returned to the table we laughed about it.

The evening continued and players' names kept being called out. Josh Kelly from the Sandringham Dragons was selected by the Giants at pick 2, which meant we would be teammates and housemates. As the draft continued past the first round, the top 10 picks were gathered in the back room for press photos.

The atmosphere was electric. We had all realised our dreams, and we laughed and chatted together about what had just happened. I was then greeted by the media manager from the Giants, who directed me through countless interviews, stretching late into the evening. I finished the night at a celebratory dinner with Leon, Graeme 'Gubby' Allan and the Giants' recruitment team, alongside my parents, Josh and his family. It had been an enormous day.

I slept poorly that night. I was buzzing with energy and excitement, and I couldn't settle. *I'm going to play in the AFL!* My alarm went off at 4.30 a.m. as I had to meet Nick Johnstone, the club's media manager, and drive 30 minutes to Coolangatta for a breakfast TV interview. The interview itself was only about ten minutes long—it hardly seemed worth the drive—and I was back at the hotel before 7 a.m. Nick called out to me as he walked away, 'See you in Sydney on Sunday.'

Sunday! It's Friday already. 'See you then!' I replied.

There was no slowing down. Our flight back to Melbourne was midmorning, and arriving in Melbourne just meant more packing and preparations to leave. We had plans to have people over on Saturday afternoon, a kind of farewell barbecue. We invited the other players from Eastern Ranges who had been drafted, and their parents—Dan McStay, who was going to Brisbane, Michael Apeness, who was going to Fremantle, and Mitch Honeychurch, who would be playing for the Bulldogs. Unfortunately, our captain, Ben Cavarra, hadn't been selected, but he was hopeful he would get an opportunity through the rookie draft. He came to my place with a huge smile, celebrating for us.

Sunday morning rolled around and my family tiptoed through the day. It was difficult to act normal with all that was going on. Dad pulled me aside and presented me with a barbecue. 'You're going to need something to cook on, mate!' he said. Mum couldn't deal with the presentation as she was too emotional. I hadn't seen her much that morning.

I felt like I couldn't get out of the house quick enough. It wasn't that I was excited to leave, but it was a painful build-up, waiting and waiting for the inevitable trip to the airport. I was nervous. It felt particularly strange to change football clubs, but it was all daunting. I wondered what my teammates would be like. I wondered if they'd like me. *How hard will preseason be, really? Am I fit enough?* I had a thousand questions running through my head on the drive to the airport, and on the plane, and when I landed. There was a car waiting for me, ready to drop me at my new apartment in Breakfast Point, organised by the club.

When I got there, I went straight to bed. All of my questions would be answered the next day, the first day of my first AFL preseason. I didn't know what the next chapter of my life would bring, but it was about to start.

6

TRAPPED

I had never seen anything like Breakfast Point. The apartment I shared with Josh Kelly and another freshly minted GWS player, Cam McCarthy, was exactly like a hundred others on our street. The neighbourhood consisted of rows and rows of townhouses, apartment blocks and houses that all looked the exact same, somehow, in a gated community filled with retirees and young families. It was a long way from the leafy eastern suburbs of Melbourne.

Our place was partly furnished, with a few staples including a coffee table and beds—just enough to make it liveable. The club arranged everything for us and would deduct the rent from our pay (or from our 'living away from home allowance', a relocation fee of sorts), so we didn't need to do a thing. This was probably for the best. At eighteen years old, with an AFL preseason looming, we had enough on our plates.

Josh and I came from relatively similar backgrounds. We had come up through the private school system, Josh having gone to Brighton Grammar and me Luther College. We had played in the Vic Metro and AIS teams together, and our parents knew each other. We weren't close friends but we were comfortable with each other—I knew what I was getting with him.

Cam was a different story, and a nice surprise. He had come over from Western Australia, and he was one of the funniest people I'd ever met. He laughed at everything and his positivity was contagious. The three of us got along well enough, considering we had been thrown together so quickly, but none of us had lived away from home before, which quickly became a challenge. We struggled to work out washing schedules, cooking schedules, how to clean up after meals and who was supposed to pay for different household items. It was your standard share-house drama, except we had had no choice about where and with whom we were living.

Our apartment was on the third floor. Below us lived another two GWS draftees, Jake Barrett and Rory Lobb. They lived with our boxing and fitness coach, Nick Walsh. None of the others had known a month in advance that they would be selected by the Giants, so they'd had a mad rush between the draft and departing for Sydney to get their lives organised, and all of it just days before preseason training started. I was lucky I'd had the chance to send my car up to Sydney. In fact, my fellow draftees were lucky too, as it was the only car we had to drive us around.

•

On the Monday after we all arrived in Sydney, preseason training got underway. I had never spent any time with a senior club before, let alone an AFL club, and the prospect was daunting. *Just keep your head down and get to work*, I thought. I was extremely conscious of seeming over-confident, so all I wanted was to fit in.

Preseason had never been my forte, plus I was coming off a major injury, so I was nervous. I'd heard many horror stories of the brutality of your first AFL preseason, so I felt wired as I arrived on that first day, alert, taking everything in. My only experience of an AFL training facility at that point was with the AIS—we'd trained at Collingwood. But the Giants' home ground felt distinctly different. For starters, our training facilities were still being built, so our rooms were in an underground athletics complex about ten minutes away on the other side of Sydney Olympic Park. It was small, crowded and extremely hot. It felt like every-one was on top of each other.

The welcome was brief. The staff introduced themselves to us and introduced us to the team, then it was a mad rush to get into our training clothes, jump in the car in our runners and boots and rush over to Tom Wills Oval and our future facilities. I was eager to train with the team, but my enthusiasm was quickly doused by the high performance staff, who had a restricted session planned for the draftees, consisting of some 200-metre shuttle runs, short kicking and skills. Primarily, we would be watching the main session.

I was uneasy. I didn't know how fit I was, or how capable my ankle injury was of withstanding the session ahead. *I'll just have to get through it*, I thought. *I can't miss the first training session.*

Josh, Cam, Jake, Rory and I all lined up to do our first set of shuttles, and everyone took off at a rate of knots, eager to impress. Josh was an elite runner already, as was Jake, and I struggled to keep up. I hung on as well as I could, determined not to be left behind. Watching the senior players train afterwards, I was in awe of the pace the ball moved at, and the speed and endurance of the players. These were the best footballers I had ever seen. It made me feel impatient. Every session I missed, my teammates were getting ahead of me, and I wanted nothing more than to get out on the field to train with them.

That afternoon brought another round of the usual athletic profiling: height, weight, skinfolds, maximum bench press, maximum bench pull. I held my breath as my weight reading came in. *102 kilograms . . . Not bad.* I had only eaten a light meal the night before and hadn't had breakfast. I was happy. My skinfolds came in at 65, which wasn't a bad start. *Plenty of time to improve*, I thought.

But for the coaches, this was above the acceptable level. I was immediately inducted into 'Fat Club', which meant a couple of extra cardio sessions a week after training. I felt a familiar rush of shame.

•

I got a handle on the training schedule soon enough. Big football training sessions Monday, Wednesday and Friday, followed by our big days lifting weights and doing Pilates, boxing and physiotherapy. Tuesday was for weights and cardio; Saturday mornings were exclusively for conditioning.

The Saturday sessions, while short, were the most daunting: two hours of brutal cardio, sometimes out at the Cronulla sand dunes, boxing sessions, CrossFit, hill sprints, you name it. My first session out at Cronulla was also the first time I vomited while exercising. I quickly learned not to eat breakfast before the Saturday sessions; there wasn't enough time to digest it before the training started.

I called Dad most days, to fill in my spare time and chat about how I was going, and every time we spoke I had the same news for him: 'That was the hardest session I have ever done.' The stories were true. An AFL preseason was brutal and exhausting.

Alongside our training regime, the first-year players had to undertake a 'Football Apprenticeship Program'. The AFL Players Association, our union, prescribed some basic education modules to test our literacy and numeracy, our financial literacy and more. I couldn't stand these sessions. The assessments weren't designed for me. I found them incredibly easy and boring, and resented the fact that we had to stay back on a Tuesday afternoon to do them, when everyone else went home.

But I did appreciate how much support we had from Melissa and Craig Lambert, the welfare staff. They assisted us with our schedules and helped us manage club expectations and any challenges we encountered. 'If you need anything, just ask,' they told us, and soon enough they were helping us with our groceries and other life admin, even helping the other boys buy cars. It didn't feel like home, but Mel and Craig gave me great support when there were things I struggled to understand.

My knowledge of other AFL clubs was limited to second-hand accounts from teammates who had been drafted the year before me, but I realised early on that the Giants were different. They were a new team, established to build a new market for the AFL in Sydney's western suburbs, where most people were more interested in the National Rugby League.

At other clubs, I would have been one of only a handful of first-round draft picks in the team, perhaps one of the only top 10 picks in the past few years, and the only number 1 pick in decades. At the Giants, who had been given preferential draft picks to help build the team, I was one of three number 1 picks, joining Jon Patton (2011) and

Lachie Whitfield (2012). Being a high draft pick wasn't rare at GWS—it was the norm. It felt like every player was highly talented, young and ultra-competitive. The club was building a list for the future and trying to improve that list as quickly as possible, and players were competing for spots against each other with a ferocity I had never seen before. It was a stark and uncomfortable change from what I was used to.

Unlike at Eastern Ranges, or at Norwood for that matter, there wasn't a sense of history or heritage at the Giants. With every session we were forging new ground. Leon was a strong communicator and often reiterated the message that if you were a third-year player, you were expected to perform consistently at the AFL level. Players who had turned eighteen in 2011 made up the majority of our list in 2013. The lack of mature players, an established team and a clear pecking order led to a sense of uncertainty, instability. I didn't know where I sat and neither did many of my teammates.

I had flourished being in the supportive environment at Eastern Ranges, but in Sydney I was dropped into a heated, competitive environment and I quickly realised that I didn't love the conflict. I liked working with people and feeling like part of a team. In Sydney, as much as we were supposed to be a team, it felt like people were working against each other, and I increasingly felt like I didn't belong. I also struggled with my own status. I wanted to be what I had been, one of the standout players, and I wanted to get there as quickly as possible.

As the weeks rolled by, I was becoming more and more exhausted. *It never stops.* Every day there was a new challenge to overcome, an unrelenting combination of physical, mental and emotional labour. We spent every waking minute living and breathing football. I was surrounded by it—I even lived with my teammates. I spent my days off doing recovery work at the club, playing table tennis or watching half-price movies at the Event Cinemas around the corner from our apartment.

One day at training, Leon pulled me and Josh to the front to applaud us for our professionalism. 'Every day off, they are here doing recovery for the next session, and they are first-years!' he said.

I was embarrassed. It wasn't that I didn't appreciate the compliment, but it felt disingenuous—I was only coming in because I had nothing else to do. I didn't know anyone in Sydney other than players and staff from the club, so I frequently called people back home to stay connected. It was refreshing to hear how other people's lives were going. Everyone I trained with was doing the same thing.

My best family friend, Brevin Campbell, had been sent to Perth for work and was experiencing many of the same challenges as me. We had vastly different jobs but we were both living with strangers in a foreign place, so we understood each other's predicament. I started calling him every week. 'There's not much to do outside of work,' he would say. 'Have you been surfing much?' I decided to bring my surfboards up to Sydney after Christmas. I needed some-thing to do other than football.

•

Before breaking for Christmas, we had a gruelling camp in Noosa—five days of the most punishing training we would face for the entire preseason. It had only been six or seven weeks since I finished school, and five or six weeks since the draft, but I couldn't wait to return home, see my friends and catch up with my family. I just had to survive the camp first.

My body had changed rapidly since I got to Sydney. I had put on muscle thanks to the four weights sessions I was doing each week, and I had improved my running. Before and after each training session we would weigh in on the scales, using the difference to determine how much fluid we needed to drink to return to a decent level of hydration.

I weighed in as usual before our first session in Noosa, and saw a bigger number than usual pop up: 108 kilograms. My weight had been steadily increasing since I joined the club, but so had my strength and fitness. I had been filling out the measurements form multiple times a week, and hadn't thought anything of it. But suddenly people were chatting about how heavy I was—including the coach.

'A hundred and eight kilos?' Leon shook his head, like he couldn't believe what he was seeing.

I hung my head. *What did I do wrong?* I had been following the program I was given to the letter. I thought I was heading in the right direction—I was running better, lifting heavier weights, progressing. I had felt good. But all the positive feelings surrounding my progress disappeared in that moment, and I felt like a failure once more.

Arriving back in Melbourne was a relief. I could escape the noise and stress of my first block of preseason training. At home, I was myself again. Everyone wanted to catch up, to ask about how training had been and to get my predications for my first AFL season.

'What's training like?'

'Who are the best players?'

'How's Sydney?'

I answered the questions the same each time: 'Tough, but I'm enjoying it . . . can't wait for games . . . Jeremy Cameron is unbelievable . . . Yeah, not bad, settled in now.' The quicker I could end the conversations about football, the better. I couldn't escape football in Sydney, so I didn't want it invading my life in Melbourne as well.

The day after Christmas, reality hit me like a tonne of bricks: *I've got to go back.* The freedom of a few days at home quickly gave way to a sense of dread. I had a personal best target for the three-kilometre time trial on our first day back, 11:15. I had never even got close to that before. I spent the rest of the holidays fretting about what I weighed and what I ate. My family went down to the house in Anglesea as usual, and I returned to my new summer routine of running, gym and extra cardio sessions, prescribed this time by the club to try to decrease my weight.

I'd wake up and go to sleep each day feeling like I was sliding towards the inevitable return flight, and I was filled with angst. The thought of going back made me so uneasy. I spoke to Dad briefly about how I was feeling, and he said, 'This is how it is, mate. You've got to knuckle down.'

He was right. My life was waiting for me in Sydney. I felt trapped.

•

The first day back at training was hot—I was even sweating on my way into the club that morning. After two weeks away, it felt like preseason was starting all over again. In the warm-up for the time trial, my back seized up, pain shooting down my leg. I was horrified. *Oh no! If I don't run, they're going to think I'm faking an injury*, I thought. *But what happens if I run badly?* I stretched and rolled my back and hips out as much as possible. *I don't have a choice.*

I did the best run of my life. It took every ounce of energy to finish, and I put in a huge effort to chase down James Stewart in the final stretch, falling agonisingly short of beating him. It didn't matter—I got the time. I finished in 11:07, taking a full minute and a half off my previous best of 12:39.

I was stoked. My time was nowhere near the best of the other players—I was a full two minutes behind Tom Scully, who had nearly broken nine minutes—but it was a massive relief to me. No one else seemed to notice, I had built up this run to mean everything, but by the time it was over, the coaches had moved on. The next training session was about to begin.

Football training had been my favourite part of the preseason. I relished the competitive drills, mucking around with my teammates and improving my goalkicking. It felt as similar to being back in the juniors as anything I could remember. I was performing well, and my improved strength and running ability meant I was feeling confident.

We began to progress into match simulation and practice games, and it was then that things began to go downhill for me. I felt lost. My teammates weren't kicking me the ball, no matter how hard I yelled for it, and I began to get frustrated. I couldn't kick goals if they didn't get me the ball.

Leon pulled me aside to chat about my progress. 'Tom, you've been going really well,' he said. 'You and Josh in particular have been progressing really well.'

I was chuffed to hear him say that.

Leon continued: 'But you haven't been getting as involved in the games as we would like.'

I explained how I was feeling—my frustration at not having the ball kicked to me.

Leon looked me in the eyes and said, 'You're not in the

juniors here, Tom. You need to prove to your teammates that you're the right option.'

I wished desperately that he was wrong, but he wasn't. I began to lose confidence in my ability. For the first time on the field, I felt completely lost.

As preseason progressed, I struggled with the intensity of the club, the unrelenting pressure of training and my inability to live a normal life. I started driving to the Northern Beaches on my days off, in search of surf and a break from everything.

Phil Davis, our captain, invited me out for coffee one day to see how I was doing. 'You don't seem to be spending much time with your teammates,' he observed.

My teammates often had breakfast together or went out at night to have fun, and it was true that I wasn't often part of the group. Phil implied that I came off as stand-offish, like I didn't want to spend time with them.

A rush of embarrassment came over me. *It's not about them*, I thought. *It's about me.* I had spent countless hours thinking about how not to come across like I thought too highly of myself, but my insecurities and unhappiness had done the job for me. *Does everyone think I'm up myself?* I spent my days off trying to get some space from everything football—I was trying to clear my head. It wasn't because I didn't like my teammates.

I tried to articulate to Phil what I was going through, but I didn't understand it myself. I felt helpless. *Why do*

I feel this way? This is what I've always wanted. It should be incredible. But I had never felt so tired or so isolated in my life. *There's something wrong with me.* My insecurities began to trouble me more and more, and racing thoughts began to invade my sleep.

•

I spoke to my manager, Liam Pickering, every so often about how I was going and what was happening in Sydney. He had mentioned at Christmas that he was coming up to Sydney in January, so we organised to have lunch at the cafe around the corner from my apartment. There, he presented me with a two-year contract extension offer from the Giants on top of the two years I already was contracted for.

I was shocked—it seemed ridiculous. I hadn't even played an AFL game! 'How can I possibly re-sign?' I asked. 'I've only been here for a couple of months. I don't know what I want to do in two weeks, let alone two years.'

Two more years with GWS would mean I was stuck in Sydney until the end of 2017. The idea of that made me feel sick.

Thankfully, Liam agreed that as good as the offer was, it wasn't the right time.

My relationship with Liam and my other manager, James, was distant. I didn't share anything personal with them, or the struggles I was having at the club. I would share how

I was travelling with Dad, but still I tried to hide the frustration and doubt I was feeling. On one of our regular phone calls, I told Dad I didn't like Sydney.

'Well, that's the reality of it right now,' he answered. Dad's feeling was that there was no use spending time on problems you couldn't solve.

He wasn't wrong—I couldn't do anything to change it. But I couldn't shake the feeling that my AFL journey wasn't turning out the way I'd thought it would. I felt like I was doing something I hadn't signed up for, even though I had been preparing for it my entire life. *Would it be different, playing in Victoria? Is Sydney the problem?* In my darker moments, another thought crept in: *Do I want play at all?* I had so many questions and no answers, and the season hadn't even begun.

•

The AFL practice matches were approaching, and the pressure at training was ramping up, but my performances in our scratch matches hadn't improved. I did well in all the training drills, but I couldn't find any form in our games. I was selected to play a half against Adelaide at Blacktown, our opening practice match, and I was equal parts nervous and excited. I had some good moments in the game, kicked a goal and felt relatively comfortable, but I wasn't selected to play the week after, nor for the match after that. I wasn't selected for our Round 1 match against the Sydney Swans.

Unlike some other clubs, the Giants had options in the tall forward department. Jeremy Cameron and Jon Patton were two years older than me, and fitter, stronger and more prepared. There was some chat about playing the three of us together, and whether that would ever be possible. It dawned on me that unless one of them got injured or they played the three of us together, I wouldn't be getting a game in the seniors.

Every game and training session that didn't go my way felt like another kilo to carry on my back. I knew that whatever I was doing wasn't working, but I didn't know why. I was fitter and stronger than I'd ever been before, but I couldn't seem to get my teammates to kick me the ball. I was always too close or too far—when I tried a short lead, the ball would go long, and vice versa. I began to get exasperated by the lack of connection I had with my team.

In the past the ball had always come to me; now it seemed to be repulsed by me. I was also tiring quickly, and began to feel unfit compared to my opponents. It didn't matter how strong I had become; I was too exhausted to use it. I started obsessing more and more over my performance, my thoughts racing long into the night, so that often I would only have had a few hours of sleep. I was so tired. And I just didn't want to think about football.

•

The 2014 AFL season continued without me. I began to play with the reserves side in the NEAFL—the North East Australian Football League—and we had great coaches in Brett Hand and Amon Buchanan. Amon and I spent countless hours working on my marking and handballing, and doing extra touch work, but I couldn't shake my feeling of disconnection.

I had never played reserves before. We operated on our own schedule, playing at different times and at different venues from the senior team. Sometimes it was hard to remember we were a part of the AFL club at all. The games were completely different to the AFL matches I'd seen. The grounds were smaller and muddier, and the competition was weaker, but somehow that didn't seem to help me play much better.

Early games against AFL-aligned teams such as Sydney felt relatively normal. I kicked four goals in my opening game, playing quite well. But as the NEAFL season progressed, we played more games against teams who were far inferior to us, and in those games I struggled to find any rhythm. The erratic nature of these games was foreign to me, and almost all the best players were midfielders.

The football media was noticeably quieter in Sydney than in Melbourne. Before I was drafted, I'd seen countless feature articles about me in major newspapers, interviews on radio and segments on television. In Sydney, the news was filled with the latest results from the NRL; we were lucky if there was one page in the newspapers covering football.

Yet even with the reduced coverage, I began to hear doubts over my performances. If my games received any coverage, my performance was inevitably described as 'disappointing'. Friends would ask me when I was going to play my first AFL game. 'How are you performing in the reserves?' They had good intentions, and they were excited for me, but I felt ashamed anyway. I couldn't shake the feeling that I was not accomplishing what I wanted to. I was frustrated both at myself and at the circumstances I found myself in. I hated playing in the reserves, despite the fact that most weeks we would win by ten goals.

Round 3 of the NEAFL season had us travelling down to Canberra to play against Belconnen, a team that—on paper at least—was far inferior to us. It was a strange feeling turning up to a local ground after having trained for the past few months in distinctly better facilities. The ground was boggy and slippery underfoot, an odd thing to see in April. I felt like I was running out for Norwood.

In the warm-up, Gubby Allan, our football operations manager, came over to me, and with a certain vigour in his voice told me that after playing well the week previously, I needed to play well again to get an opportunity at the top level. 'Play well today, put your name in the ring for next week,' he said.

I was inspired. I relished the challenge, and I was determined to prove Gubby right. The day went just as I had hoped—I played well, kicking straight and marking well—and I thought about what Gubby had said on the drive home. *Am I really a chance?*

I didn't want to be too optimistic, fearing disappointment, but my hopes were confirmed by Leon on the Wednesday afternoon. 'We're going to play you this week, mate,' he told me. 'You've been close and had a couple of good games.'

I was quietly thrilled, but I didn't want to be distracted. *Getting picked is just the beginning—now I've got to play well,* I thought. The game would be against the Crows at the Adelaide Oval, one of the first games back at the revamped historic stadium.

As happy as I was at the prospect of playing in my first AFL game, being a part of the AFL squad for a training week was just as exciting. There was no game for the reserves that weekend, so they would be training separately. All of the club's resources gravitated towards me and the AFL side— more treatment, more preparation from coaches, more smiles and good wishes from the staff. I had experienced the other side of the coin as a reserves player, where you felt like a ghost walking through the building, so it was strange to feel like one of the 'cool kids'.

When I rang my parents to let them know in advance that I would be debuting, Dad responded in his typically even-handed way: 'Getting selected is only the beginning.' Mum was a little more effusive: 'Well done, Tom, I'm so proud of you!'

They booked a flight to Adelaide, along with my friends Mark, Andy and Molly, who were all keen to share in this amazing moment in my career.

•

All that was left to do now was play the game. I was quietly confident, but had no idea what to expect. After the first four games of the AFL season, the Giants had two wins and two losses, but there was plenty of optimism in the building after the club's difficult first two seasons. Our list had matured and it looked like we could finally compete with the best, week on week. It gave me confidence to know that we were in a reasonable spot. *If I can just get a few chances, I'll be okay*, I thought. An Adelaide mistake here, a good contest there and I'd be able to build a good game.

We travelled over to Adelaide the day before the game and I finally got to witness all the little kinks and idiosyncrasies of my teammates on the way. Some read, some played cards, some sat by themselves and some had to be in a group. With so many young men from so many different walks of life, it was a melting pot of personalities.

Checking in at the hotel was relatively uneventful, barring the fact that I realised, as a senior player, I had the privilege of my own hotel room. This was a first. We had a light training session at Adelaide Oval, and a team meeting and dinner, and then I closed my eyes for the last time before becoming an AFL player.

The next day it seemed like Adelaide had come alive. We drove to the ground in the team bus, through droves of fans, although none of them were there to see us. Mum and Dad were in the rooms before the game to witness me being presented with my first jumper. *This is real*, I thought. *I'm an AFL player*. But I didn't have time to dwell on the moment, as the focus quickly shifted away from me.

It was going to take a strong team effort to win. We prepared to run out onto the field, into the glare of the bright lights and TV cameras, and lined up across from me were players of genuine stardom: Patrick Dangerfield, Taylor Walker and Rory Sloane, just to name a few. My nerves sharpened. I thought about every little moment on the path to this one, every time I had played this scenario through in my head, and then we headed up the race to play.

'*Boooo!*' The crowd was electric, and they were sending nothing but negative energy our way. I had never played at a ground with such a big crowd, let alone one this hostile. Our captain, Callan Ward, brought our attention back, over and over again. 'It's about us!' he yelled.

Game on. The speed shocked me. The ball whizzed around so quickly, the players moved faster than anything I'd seen, and before long I was completely gassed. As forwards, we had very few opportunities—an early marking opportunity in the forward 50 went begging. A small fumble here and I began to worry. *This is not going well.*

The crowd was vicious, hurling abuse my way.

'Embarrassing, Boyd!'

'Number 1 draft pick? You're shit!'

There was no avoiding it. I tried to stay in the game, but their voices were booming in my head.

By half time things were looking disastrous: eleven goals to three, Adelaide's way. We were getting dominated through the middle of the ground and I felt completely lost. I tried to stay focused during the break, listening hard to the coaches, but inside I was bewildered.

The second half wasn't much better. It was hard to imagine things being more difficult. Every disposal I got felt amazing, but there weren't many. The final score read Adelaide 21.11 (137), the Giants 10.12 (72). I'd had only five disposals, and no goals. It was a disaster.

A range of thoughts and emotions went through me following the game. *It's not my fault*, I told myself. *You didn't play well, though*, my mind countered. I couldn't absolve myself of blame, because I hadn't been a part of the solution, and we were resoundingly beaten. *Surely they can't drop me after one week?* I wondered, but I wasn't convinced.

I forgot about the struggles of the day briefly so I could enjoy the company of my family and friends. Playing a senior match was a milestone to be happy about, regardless of the result. But on the bus ride back to the airport, the distraction of my friends and family faded away, and I became more and more aware that a long and difficult season lay ahead of me.

7

DESPERATION

The review of my first AFL game wasn't pretty. Leon was clear that we weren't good enough, and that if players couldn't play their role to an acceptable level, then there were 'plenty of players playing good football in the NEAFL' to take our place.

Surely he doesn't mean me? I thought. *That was only my first game, and we got smashed. What was I supposed to do? It's not my fault.*

Playing reserves had been foreign to me, but moving in and out of the senior side was completely unfathomable. I'd never had to fight for my spot from week to week. I'd never even been in consideration to be dropped, in my entire football career.

My individual review meeting with Leon was eye-opening. He walked me through some of the things I had done during the game, and told me what I could have done better in those moments.

'So, Tom, that's the end of your tape. There are some good things in there, but we need more involvement from you.'

I dreaded his next sentence. *Please don't drop me!*

Leon continued. 'Honestly, it's not up to AFL standard, but we are going to stick with you this week—we want to see you have another go.'

Relief flooded through me. I didn't feel attacked, but Leon was clear: he needed more from me, and from my teammates. The challenge was simple, and consistent with what he'd said to the entire team: 'If you aren't up to it, we will find someone who is.'

Our next game would take place on the Gold Coast. It was built up as a significant match on our fixture—'The two newest teams in the competition go head to head!' There were high expectations that we would win the game and upset the slightly older, slightly more experienced Gold Coast Suns.

I amped myself up as much as I could to perform well. *I'm going to show them what I can do! I'm going to prove myself!* But I could feel my skin burning and I was sweating profusely as the game started. It was so hot up in Queensland. I had to play well—Dan McStay had even come down from Brisbane to support me—but already the pressure was getting the better of me.

The game was fierce from the beginning, sweat and bodies flying everywhere in the sticky Gold Coast heat. I got my opportunity with a high ball coming my way early in the first quarter—I bodied my man out, and my eyes lit up. *This is going to be my first goal!*

Then *clunk!* Agony. As I reached out my hands to mark the ball, a body collided full-speed into my right arm, dislocating my shoulder. I fell to my knees and heard myself groan. It was one of the most painful things I'd ever felt in my life. *Not now*, I thought in disbelief. *How could this be happening now?*

I struggled to my feet as the doctors rushed out to assist me. I couldn't lift my arm. Tim Parham, the team physio, helped me off the field and into the rooms to assess the damage. He moved my arm, testing my stability and strength as I winced and caught my breath.

'You've hurt your posterior shoulder,' he concluded.

'Is it bad? How long will I be out?' I asked.

'We'll get it scanned after the game, but for now we need you back out there.'

I couldn't believe what he was saying. 'How am I supposed to play? I can't even lift my arm.'

But in the AFL there are ways. I had some painkillers and Tim strapped my shoulder, tightly, and sent me back out to the bench.

The rest of the game was a write-off. I had just two disposals; I couldn't handball, mark or kick. I couldn't really do anything, as least not the way I wanted to. One of my two disposals was a horrendous attempt at handballing to an open Jeremy Cameron—before I connected with the ball, my shoulder tape stopped me short, leaving me swinging my clenched fist at fresh air. Jezza wasn't happy, and I was incredibly frustrated. I was obviously not right to play. I'd never had a shoulder injury, but I was sure it wasn't good. I felt like cannon fodder.

It was some relief to be subbed out of the game at three-quarter time, though soon I began to dread time on the sidelines, or worse to be dropped and have to play injured in the reserves.

The flight home and the days following were incredibly painful. By Wednesday, I was sitting in a surgeon's office with MRI results and X-rays in front of me. 'You're going to need surgery to repair the damage to the back of your shoulder,' the surgeon said matter-of-factly.

I asked him immediately, 'What's the recovery time?' and he told me—sixteen weeks. I let out a long breath and thought, *My season is over*. I was disappointed, but I was also relieved. At least I knew that the injury was serious—I hadn't struggled so badly for no reason.

'It's funny,' the surgeon continued, 'we usually don't see AFL players with this injury, it's usually the rugby players.'

Driving back to the football club, I called Dad to give him the news: 'Yep, surgery. I'll be out for sixteen weeks.' Back at the club, I sat down with Leroy Lobo, the head physio, expecting to learn my surgery date. There was no mention of it.

'Okay, Tom, here is the strength program we're going to put you on, which is going to help protect that shoulder,' Leroy said.

What? I was confused. *Have I missed something? Did I misunderstand the surgeon?*

'But don't I need surgery?' I asked. 'I thought I needed to get it fixed.'

Leroy explained that many AFL players had similar injuries, and that if they fixed it immediately, I would miss the entire season, so they were going to help me 'manage it' instead. 'We'll review it at the end of the year and see how you are then.'

Leroy had been a great supporter of mine and I trusted his judgement, but I felt really uncertain about this. I didn't think I had misunderstood the surgeon. If I ignored his advice, was I going to injure myself further and cause long-lasting damage? *Is this normal?* I had to adjust my entire conception of what an injury was in the space of five minutes, and accept that the reality was that I was going to be playing the remainder of the season with a damaged shoulder. It would require fixing at some stage, but not at a time that was inconvenient to the club. I would play the following week, but I'd be back in the reserves.

I was beyond disappointed. My injury had prevented me from playing well in the AFL, and now I was going to have to play with the same injury in the twos. I dreaded the thought.

•

After my two disappointing games with the AFL side, my season began to lose momentum. My performances at the lower level were not better—I was always a kick away from the marking contest, then the next ball would go over my head. I was always out on my own when a mistake would happen, and I would be left out of the play. The grounds were too small, the conditions were poor and my frustration was only building.

I couldn't help but think that I would be better at AFL level—that those two games I'd played in the senior team were just anomalies. *After all, we got pumped both games.* I was sure things would improve if I could just get out of the NEAFL. It wasn't my fault that I was playing poorly—the competition didn't suit me.

I was hopeful of a return to the AFL side—after all, GWS made more changes from week to week than any other team in the competition, or so it felt. On a bad week at Eastern Ranges, we would change maybe three or four players, mainly due to injury, but every week the Giants would swap out five players or more, just to change the dynamic. I could see it playing on my teammates' minds in the NEAFL, particularly those in the midfield. Players would be fighting and

scrapping for more midfield time, trying to get more posses-
sions and sometimes not coming off the ground when they
were told. Their desperation to perform was like nothing
I had ever seen, and it made me really uneasy.

I longed for the days at my previous clubs, where
everyone was trying to help each other, where individual
improvement didn't come at the cost of someone else, and
where there was a high degree of support. The happiest
players at GWS were the ones who played reserves every
week, where they had some consistency and structure to
follow. The ones who were struggling were in and out of
the AFL side, and always seemed to be left feeling bitter
and frustrated.

I was frustrated too, especially having glimpsed how well
the AFL team was catered for. While the AFL team would
fly to Canberra, we had to drive. Where the AFL team had
their own hotel room, we shared. The staff were limited in
the NEAFL competition, so we had less support. We were
second-class citizens. I began to get distracted by all these
petty details, which felt to me like obstacles in the way of
my success.

But no matter what I told myself, the truth was that
my performances simply weren't good. And I couldn't get
to grips with the reality that I wasn't playing well. Senior
football was more challenging than my junior games: it was
more defensive, and the players were fitter, stronger, faster.
I was slow and heavy; my weight played on my mind before

every game, and soon I began to skip weighing in altogether. If I was forced to do it, I would jump off the scales quickly, refusing to see or acknowledge the number. I wanted to train hard to lose weight, but I was sleeping poorly—a handful of hours every night, at best—so I was exhausted all the time. I didn't understand what was happening to me.

Why was I feeling so off? Why was I so uncomfortable and jittery all the time? *Why can't I sleep?* I was scared of what was going on inside me, but I couldn't explain the way I was feeling to anyone. I just didn't feel like *me*. Who was I really going to tell, anyway? Everyone who really knew me was back in Victoria, and I began to wish I was still there too. I only knew that I had to keep pushing—I had a job to do and I couldn't let anyone down.

•

After a few weeks in the reserves, I felt more disconnected than ever before from any sense of purpose. I was no longer talking to the AFL forwards coach, Alan McConnell. Leon hadn't said anything more than hello to me for a few weeks, and I was feeling left out. I wanted to know that I still mattered.

I attempted some humour with Alan a couple of times: 'You don't say much to me anymore! Remember me?' I wanted him to know that I was still there, still committed to playing seniors, but it backfired. Leon pulled me into his office for a chat. 'So you're unhappy playing reserves? Do you think you should be playing AFL?'

I felt sick to my stomach—this wasn't what I wanted. I realised that I had come off as petty and entitled. Longing for the attention of the coaches of the AFL side had just made me look immature and desperate.

'You're not playing good enough to be picked at the moment,' Leon said frankly. 'In fact, some of your team-mates in the NEAFL are in front of you.' He clearly thought I needed a reality check.

Wow, I've really screwed this up, I thought. With my tail between my legs, I went back to the reserves, feeling like a scolded child, but something shifted. Brett Hand and Amon Buchanan took me under their wing. We chatted about where I needed to improve and made a few changes. So in a way, the conversation with Leon had led to a good result. I needed to grow up, I needed to get better, and this was how I was going to do it.

They added extra training sessions to strengthen my shoulder and improve my skills, and moved my focus from weight training to cardio to change my body composition. I also met with the team dietician. I was grateful for the support, but at some level it was overwhelming. I thought I was good enough, but I wasn't, and I needed to take control of changing that.

With the season rolling on, I noticed that criticism of me in the media was growing. It was implied, not direct:

'Where is the number 1 draft pick?' 'Why is he not performing?' 'Is he injured?' Less than a year earlier, the same people had been singing my praises, and now they were speculating about whether I was of any value at all. It hurt.

I knew many of these people. I had talked to a lot of them, and thought we'd got along well. I longed for an excuse, something that would explain why I was having such an underwhelming season. *Can I blame the grounds? The competition? The weather? My shoulder?* Every option felt weak and shameful. I tried to ignore the press, and the comments on social media, but their doubt was infectious. I could sense frustration from my teammates too, like I was letting them down, but I couldn't tell how much of it was real and how much of it was in my head.

To make matters worse, after weeks of me playing in the reserves side, a batch of Gatorade bottles arrived for me at the club with my face on the side of each bottle. Some months earlier, I had signed a deal to be featured on the drinks, alongside players such as Gary Ablett, Scott Pendlebury and Luke Parker. Three of the four featured players were superstars of the game, and then there was me, the number 1 draft pick. I was supposed to be a future star, but it wasn't working out that way.

I copped some friendly heckling from my teammates, and I laughed and smiled in response—*What a joke!* But their critique was accurate. I was a disappointment.

For every self-critical thought I had, I tried to combat it

internally either by ignoring it or by trying to convince myself that it wasn't true. I was stuck on a merry-go-round of doubt, frustration and blame, laying it either on myself or on others. I wanted so badly to do well, and I hated letting people down. I just wanted to make others happy. I was trying, but I couldn't. I wasn't good enough, and so I was unhappy.

As the weeks passed, I became exceedingly uncomfortable around the football club. The time I spent there made me anxious. I struggled to feel like I belonged, and I was constantly worried about what other people thought of me. Training was always enjoyable, but once the endorphins had worn off I quickly fell back into feelings of self-doubt and disillusion. Long, sleepless nights were followed by groggy mornings. I began to wonder if there was something wrong with me, and if it would ever end. I was usually too tired to socialise, and so I began to turn down offers to spend time with my teammates; after a while those offers stopped coming. I spent my days off alone, looking for any activity to distract me from how things were going at the club.

I missed home, my parents, my friends and my old life. My parents came up to Sydney quite regularly (Dad often came up for work, which was great) but my time with them always felt borrowed. We were never together for more than a short time before they had to go back to Melbourne. It felt unnatural, like we were together because we had to be, not because we wanted to be.

My younger sister Tessa used my games as an excuse to get her L-plate hours up, driving Dad up to see me play in Canberra. It was always nice to see them, but we would rarely get any more than a few moments together before I had to jump on a bus back to Sydney. *It's better than nothing*, I thought. I was thankful for their company; I knew everything would have been even worse if I were alone the entire time.

Conversations with friends back home always went the same way—'Is it great?' 'How are your teammates?' 'Are you going to play again soon?'—but after a while they dropped away. Brevin was one of the only people I really spoke to about how I was going, and he was on the other side of the country.

I had conflicting feelings about how little I was seeing my teammates. On the one hand, I was so wrung out from the effort of gritting my teeth and smiling through a day at the club that I was shattered by the time we were done. On the other hand, I was lonely. The weeks were getting more difficult. I spent hours in my room, or off on my own, barely talking to anyone. I constantly felt unwell, exhausted. *When is this going to end?*

•

Somehow I managed to scrape together a couple of decent performances in the NEAFL, and then the senior team's star full-forward, Jeremy Cameron, went down with an injury. And so in Round 14, against all expectation, I got another chance. I was desperate to make it work this time. *Hopefully Jezza gives me a couple of weeks to settle in*, I thought.

Running out onto the field for the game against Carlton, I felt better, more involved. Things didn't feel as fast as they had in my first two AFL games. I found a rhythm. I kept looking over to the bench, hoping, praying that I didn't get subbed out of the game. When the fourth quarter began, we were in front and I could sense my first win. I hadn't been subbed out—things were looking up! Minutes into the quarter, I got on the end of a scrubbed kick in the goal square, and with one hand threw the ball onto my boot. *Yes!* My first goal in the AFL was an important one, extending our lead. The final quarter was close, and stressful, but we came out on top. I couldn't believe it. I couldn't wipe the grin off my face when the final siren sounded.

My first AFL win felt like a dream come true. My team-mates showered me in Gatorade, congratulated me, and I suddenly felt like I was a part of something again. It was the happiest I'd felt in months.

I tried to hold on to that feeling in the days following the game, but the joy of winning was quickly washed away by a wave of doubt about my performance. *Was it good enough?* I tried to read cues on the faces of the people around me.

The mood at the club was completely different to anything I'd experienced previously. The win had put a smile on everyone's face, and I welcomed the increased positivity in the building. I convinced myself that I was probably safe in the team—*I was part of the winning team!* And anyway, it didn't look like Jeremy Cameron was going to be fit to play. I really liked Jezz—he was good fun to be around and I looked up to him—but secretly I was glad to hear that he wasn't in the clear. My spot in the side appeared safe.

Everything changed that Thursday afternoon. I trained with the senior team, but before the end of the day Leon called me to his office.

'You were better on the weekend, Tom,' he told me. 'I thought it was a good step forward, but Jeremy is going to play this week.'

Of course, I thought. *Of course*. I was shattered. I left his office dejected, but it quickly morphed into anger. *What did I miss? Nothing!* Jeremy was injured—he hadn't trained. *This is completely unfair*, I seethed. Minutes later I rejoined the reserves side for a team meeting, and settled back into the anonymity of the NEAFL for another weekend.

•

A month passed and I became increasingly miserable. *I don't want to do this anymore*, I thought constantly. Football wasn't working out the way I'd wanted it to. I was impatient for success and annoyed by my situation. I didn't enjoy anything about playing reserves. I liked my teammates, but the games felt soulless. I hated having to hope that players in the AFL side would play poorly or get injured, to make way for me to play. It didn't feel good.

I began to long for a move home to Victoria. I wanted a fresh start, a new environment, something to help me feel better about myself. I wanted to run away, to move clubs, or else to find some magical solution to the problems I was having in Sydney. *Why can't I sleep? Why am I feeling sick and nervous all the time? Why is everything so frustrating?* My thoughts spiralled. *I don't want to play football anymore.*

My racing mind kept me up at night and stressed me out during the day. I felt cornered, scared and completely unsure how to change the situation. The only thing I could look forward to was the bye round, when I could go home for a few days, and then finally, at the end of the year, my first off-season.

My parents were worried. I couldn't hide how I was feeling from them—it was written all over my face when they visited. They tried calling more and visiting more, but it was hard with my busy schedule. I know that Mum, in particular, was incredibly concerned.

After a NEAFL game one week, Dad called me to tell me he was coming to visit. 'I've got something I need to talk to you about,' he said. I was perplexed—what could he possibly have to tell me that couldn't be done over the phone? But he insisted, so we organised to catch up a few days later. Dad would fly up to Sydney and we would have dinner together.

We sat down at the Palace Hotel, a local pub, and we both ordered a steak. Dad hadn't said much. 'So, what did you want to talk about?' I asked.

He didn't respond straightaway. He set his jaw, preparing to deliver something serious. 'Tom, you've received a contract offer,' Dad said.

I stiffened. Why had he come all this way to tell me this? 'I don't want to re-sign with the Giants right now, Dad, I want to wait,' I said firmly. *What is he thinking? He knows how unhappy I am here*, I thought gruffly.

'It's not from the Giants,' Dad replied.

This caught me off-guard. 'Well, who's it from?'

'The Western Bulldogs.'

I had been surprised; now I was interested. The Western Bulldogs had shown a lot of interest in me ahead of the draft. I had spoken to their list manager, Jason McCartney, a number of times. I liked him. 'What's the offer?' I asked.

Dad paused. 'Seven over seven,' he said quietly.

'Seven hundred thousand a year for seven years?' I was shocked. That was a huge deal, much bigger than I had anticipated. I was trying to process what that sort of contract would mean for my life, but Dad stopped me.

'No, not seven hundred thousand—seven million over seven years.'

My heart nearly came out of my chest. This offer was insane. But it wasn't the money itself that made me smile— the size of the deal was a sign of how much they wanted me.

My mind was quickly drawn to the idea of being the number one forward at the Bulldogs, having a whole club backing me, and especially being back in Victoria. I longed for all these things. It seemed too good to be true. I would have signed the deal right then if it was in front of me. But was it even possible? I'd been drafted by the Giants, and I had signed a two-year rookie contract. And with it came the expectation that I would continue playing for them.

'What do we do from here?' I asked impatiently.

'Well, I've spoken to Pickers, and I think we should at least meet with them,' Dad told me. 'You're still under contract, at least for another eighteen months, so it will be difficult, but opportunities like this don't come around often.'

Instantly my enthusiasm deflated. The reality of how challenging it would be to take up this offer began to dawn on me. I wanted it so badly, but that didn't mean it was going to happen. My mind wandered, and a now-familiar sickness set in, my heart beginning to pound. *I want to go back home. Will the Giants let me go? What will my teammates think of me? I can't stay here.*

By the time our dinner was over, Dad and I had hatched a plan to meet with the Bulldogs back in Melbourne during the split round later in the year. I needed to hear what they had to say. *If they want me, then they must think there's a way they can make it happen.*

•

The week before I was due to meet with the Bulldogs, I returned to the senior side for the Giants, playing Geelong at Sydney Olympic Park. I played a dismal first half. I couldn't stop worrying about being subbed out and the disappointment that would come with it.

Leon approached me at three-quarter time. 'We can't take you out and we need more from you,' he challenged me. 'C'mon!'

I knew I deserved the spray, and I set myself for a big final quarter. My first contest was a good one—a mark and goal. That gave me a rush, and I kept fighting through the last moments of a close game. With four minutes to go, I grabbed another contested mark and kicked another goal, putting us within seven points of the Cats.

Immediately afterwards, a perfect kick came my way and I stretched out, winning a free kick 40 metres out and directly in front of the goals. I took a deep breath. This was the game and performance that I had been waiting for.

I calmly walked back, lined up for goal and kicked—it looked dead straight. My heart skipped a beat. 'Yes!' hissed the crowd, but then, 'No!' The ball had faded sharply. My tired legs didn't have the power to kick true.

I was gutted—it was my moment, but I had fallen short. We'd come close but ultimately we'd lost, and the biggest missed opportunity was mine.

My mind quickly moved to the meeting I had in the week ahead. My good performance gave me the confidence boost

I needed. I had just played my best quarter of AFL football, and I was about to be offered the deal of a lifetime.

•

Returning to Melbourne felt strange this time. Previously I had felt a kind of longing—now I had hope, excitement. *I might be back here soon!*

Dad and I met with Liam Pickering in Richmond to discuss the meeting ahead, then we left the cafe together and drove to the home of the Bulldogs' president, Peter Gordon.

'Who's going to be there?' I asked. I was nervous. I realised how out of my depth I would be in this conversation—just a kid trying to make decisions for the future of an adult.

'The coach, the CEO, the president and the list manager,' Liam replied.

Whoa, okay. All the club's top leaders would be at this secret meeting. My nerves tightened again.

Liam must have sensed it. 'Don't worry, mate, this is about them, not so much about you. I'll run the conversation.'

Liam was a veteran of deals like this, having orchestrated some of the biggest trades in AFL history—although no eighteen-year-old footballer had ever been offered a million dollars a year before.

When we arrived at Peter's home—one of the nicest houses I'd ever seen—we were ushered to an upstairs living room. A small group was waiting for us: Simon Garlick, the

Bulldogs' CEO; Jason McCartney, the list manager; Brendan McCartney, the senior coach; and of course Peter, their president. I was intimidated by the men looking at me, and not comfortable enough to say much, but I greeted each of them with a handshake and a smile, professional, polite.

We sat down and the discussion began. Much of the talk was around the future of the club; its direction, its list and the talent they already had on board. I didn't need much convincing, to be honest, but the presentation was impressive. They had a plan, and to execute it they needed a strong forward.

When the presentation concluded, the conversation got down to brass tacks, with Liam leading the way. 'So, how are we going to get this done? Because the way I see it, and I've seen a lot of these, there's only two players on your list that the Giants would trade for Tom, if you want to trade for him this year—Bontempelli and Griffen.'

The temperature in the room shifted; it became noticeably uncomfortable. Ryan Griffen was the Bulldogs' captain. *Did Pickers really just say that?* I thought, in shock.

I stayed silent, but the conversation continued around me. The Bulldogs' team was adamant that those two players were off the table. But then how could it be done? The conversation slowed as they contemplated the difficult road that lay ahead.

There was one other thing we wanted to know before the meeting was done, and Liam hadn't raised it yet. Dad, who had been uncharacteristically quiet through the meeting, spoke up. 'Look, Brendan, the presentation that you gave was terrific, and the list over the next few years looks really promising, but what I want to know is how long you're going to be there.'

I just about fell off my chair. *What a question to ask!* I was way out of my depth, but still I shrunk a little in discomfort. I was so relieved that Dad and Liam were there to lead the difficult conversation.

'Well, Geoff,' Brendan replied, 'my contract has another two years on it, so I'll be here for another two years at least.'

Not long after, the meeting adjourned and we headed back to our car. Before we even left Peter's underground car park, I launched into a debrief. 'What did you think?' I asked in excitement.

'Wait till we leave—we'll talk about it after,' Dad replied sternly.

As Dad reversed the car, there was an almighty crunch, followed by a screech. We looked around, puzzled, then saw it: Dad had torn the side mirror completely off his car. It was hanging on by its wiring, a mess of smashed glass and broken plastic. We looked up to see Liam's two daughters looking on and laughing hysterically.

Dad let out a few expletives, then Peter came down. 'Don't worry about it,' he said. 'I know a guy who can fix it—I'll be in touch.'

Dad drove home sheepishly.

•

Back in Sydney, I felt like I was living a double life. I had this big secret that I had to keep to myself. Back at the club, I tried to focus on football, reflecting on my previous performance against Geelong and what it meant for the weeks ahead. I was confident that I would hold my spot this time. *They can't drop me after that final quarter.* I wanted to feel like I was part of the team, but I also had the guilty knowledge that I might not be there long-term.

For the next few games I felt completely different. It was like I had a shield against the negativity around bad losses or poor performances—after all, my future elsewhere was secure. The knowledge that I had this enormous deal pending with the Bulldogs was like a blanket I could cover myself with when things got difficult on the field. When I was frustrated or disappointed, when the coaches weren't happy with me or the team was struggling, I could retreat to the back of my mind and avoid all the anxious thoughts that would otherwise have overwhelmed me. *I don't have to deal with this much longer.*

Meanwhile, my AFL career had never been more stable. Leon told me that I would play senior football for the rest of the year. 'You've been a bit quiet, but we're going to stick with you,' he said. That gave me the confidence to focus on playing rather than being frightened of an impending demotion. With this came a stability that I hadn't known since I'd arrived in Sydney. Suddenly I could plan my weeks and weekends, because I knew where I was and what I was going to be doing.

It wasn't all smooth sailing, however. The team had got even more competitive as the year progressed. Some players began to focus on performing well individually, trying to salvage some personal success while the team was flailing. On the field, feedback was stark and swift—I never had any doubt about what my teammates thought of me, and some players took it too far. Feedback became abuse, often with selfish intentions. One time I even managed to get abused after taking a mark and lining up for a set shot. 'Fucking handball it! Fuck me, you better kick it now!' I was 40 metres out, directly in front of the goal, and I missed. *What the hell is going on here?* I thought in frustration.

I played my first AFL games in Melbourne during this time—first against Richmond, then against Melbourne, and in our final round against the Bulldogs. These matches gave me a new perspective on the game and on my job. Being in Melbourne, staying at the Novotel on the St Kilda foreshore, meant freedom. It meant seeing my parents and being back home.

The game against the Bulldogs felt odd, almost like an audition. *How am I going to go playing against them? Does anyone on the team know about our contract discussions? Has word got out?* It was distracting and stressful to think about, so I tried to ignore any thought unrelated to playing football. It didn't work particularly well. I couldn't help but worry that someone from the Bulldogs would tell one of my teammates or coaches that I was trying to join them. *That makes no sense—they came to me*, I told myself, but it wasn't working.

The game was a fierce one, there was immediate animosity between the sides and scuffles ensued. It had much more feeling than I expected for a Round 23 game between two teams that were not going to make finals. But Bulldogs legend Daniel Giansiracusa was playing his final game before retiring, and the Bulldogs wanted to give him a good send-off.

With only minutes left in the final quarter, it looked like the game could go either way, and I was shattered. I sensed we were about to lose our grasp on the game when a long ball went inside 50, towards the Bulldogs forward Jake Stringer. He dropped a sitter and the ball spilled, heading my way. There was a lead. The ball got kicked up in the air and I ran back to mark it, but it spilled out of my reach. I gathered it up and handed it to Devon Smith, and he streamed forward with Adam Treloar, screaming at him to handball. *Goal! We win!* All thoughts about the Bulldogs offer had left my mind—I was a Giants player and we'd just won a huge game.

The after-match was comforting, a nice place to be. It was a satisfying way to end the season. 'Next year, we want to contend for finals,' Leon said. Sitting in a rare moment of football joy as we rode the bus to the airport, I tweeted my thoughts, which I felt honestly in that moment: 'A great sign of what we are building here at the Giants!'

On our return to Sydney, I was sternly reminded that my season wasn't quite done yet. The AFL side was finished, but the NEAFL side was ready to play finals, and we were positioned for a premiership. The past few weeks had been particularly challenging for me physically. Each week was harder to prepare for; with each game I played, my injuries were more difficult to ignore. It seemed impossible with a six-day turnaround to prepare for a finals match.

I hadn't played in Sydney in two months and I felt like I needed a break. I trained for the game, but the physios determined ultimately that I should sit it out, and I was relieved. I was mentally and physically spent. The reserves side was a hot favourite to win, and I would be able to play the following week in the NEAFL Grand Final, but things didn't go according to plan. The side went down to Aspley, meaning my first season with the Giants was officially done.

My mind quickly turned to a surf trip in Indonesia that I had planned. All I had to do before I left Sydney was find a new place to live. Our time at Breakfast Point was done, so my housemates and I haphazardly landed on a four-bedroom house in Concord. The last thing I did before flying home to Melbourne was sign the lease agreement.

•

In Melbourne, all I could think about was the enormous offer that was pending with the Bulldogs. I wanted nothing more than to be coming back to Victoria for good, bags packed and contract signed. But it couldn't happen, I told myself. The Giants would never just let me go. Even asking the question would create a terribly uncomfortable situation for me, stuck between a club that I didn't want to play for and a club that didn't have the means to trade for me.

With all this uncertainty, I decided the best thing was to try to forget it all, so my trip to Indonesia couldn't have come at a better time. Brevin had returned from Perth, and his housemate Aidan was going to join us on holiday, along with my friend from my Vic Metro days—now a Richmond player—Nick Vlastuin. It was exactly what I needed: sun, surfing and laughter.

Our trip took us through Kuala Lumpur, in Malaysia, then on to the city of Padang, in Indonesia, before a four-hour speedboat ride dropped us on a tiny chain of islands in the middle of the ocean called the Mentawais. All in all, it was 48 hours between us leaving Melbourne and stepping onto the Mentawai sand.

Our surf camp was run by a Columbian named Diego and his wife, Lora. Diego had spent ten years on the Gold Coast working in tourism, he told us, before relocating to the remote island of Siberut. Who could blame him? The surf in Indonesia is world-class, and Mentawai is one of the few barely touched parts of the world. Islands covered by palm trees popped out of the water every kilometre or so, surrounded by crystal clear, fish-filled water. Paradise.

Each day we got up at dawn, taking in the humidity and sun, and talked about the conditions—the wind and the swell. We would plan the day ahead, where and when we would surf, what boards we would take and how long we would surf for. There was no phone reception, no computers and no real connection to the outside world, other than a satellite phone in Diego's office and the incredibly slow wi-fi, for which he charged $50 a day. But it hardly mattered to us what was happening elsewhere. We spearfished for Spanish mackerel, surfed over coral reefs and had Bintang beers on the boat as the sun set. I had never felt so at peace.

There was just one thing we couldn't escape from. In Australia, the AFL trade period had begun, but I couldn't tell anyone about the offer I'd received. And it didn't really seem to matter. I was playing with the Giants in 2015— that seemed a certainty. Headlines from the trades would fly around the camp, and we chatted casually about what each trade meant and how it would affect our teams. I checked the trade news every morning when the wi-fi was working best, but I didn't find anything of particular importance—at least, not until 8 October came around.

That morning I logged on to the footy news, and my eyes bulged out of my head. I couldn't believe what I was reading: 'Ryan Griffen requests trade from Western Bulldogs to GWS Giants.'

My heart was pounding. *What does this mean? Who can I talk to about this? How can I contact anyone?* I had given Liam Pickering a limited power of attorney before I'd left overseas. 'Just in case something changes,' he told me. *But why would he ever need that?* Maybe Liam knew something I didn't, I now thought, because one of the biggest puzzle pieces for my trade to the Bulldogs looked like it had just shaken loose.

I was unbelievably excited, and I needed answers, but I was thousands of kilometres away from the action. I couldn't share my mental turmoil with anyone at the camp—whatever was going to happen next would need to be carefully orchestrated. *I need to talk to Liam*, I thought.

Getting through to anyone back home was a nightmare. The wi-fi was terrible; the best I could manage was to send and receive iMessages, which sometimes went through and sometimes didn't. I gleaned from Liam that the Bulldogs were ready to make the trade and Liam thought he could get it done.

I didn't know what to do. There were literally millions of dollars on the line, and the lives of at least two footballers, probably more. A whole industry of people would change with my decision. *And I'm only nineteen*, I thought. The pressure was intense.

I managed to exchange a few fleeting texts with Dad, to see what he thought of the situation. 'I can't make the decision for you,' he wrote. 'But everything that has worked out in my life, particularly in business, started when I took a risk.'

It was the advice I needed. 'Go ahead, mate,' I messaged Pickers. 'Make the deal.' Then I took a deep breath, sensing that my world was about to change in a major way.

I had remained at camp that morning while the others took the boat out in search of surf. I was grateful to be alone—I needed time to process making the biggest decision of my life, all from a hut on a tiny island in the middle of the ocean. But the boys would be coming back at some point. *What am I going to say?* I wondered. *What are they going to say?* My mind was racing.

Before long, my friends were back at camp. Aidan was the first to mount the steps into the communal lounge area. 'Any trade news?' he asked.

'Nah,' I replied. I waited quietly for the inevitable, watching Aidan as he picked up his phone and surfed the dodgy internet to find the football news. A few minutes later, he looked up at me, eyes wide. 'No trade news?!'

I laughed. Our mates quickly came over to see what the commotion was.

Brevin is a Bulldogs tragic, so he was smiling from ear to ear. 'Welcome to the kennel!' he said ecstatically.

But Nick wasn't as happy about it. 'Seven years? Seven million?' he scoffed. 'You've barely played any games!'

I was taken aback. 'What do you want me to do about it?' I said defensively. 'I didn't make the offer!'

Nick came around quickly and was genuinely happy for me, and soon we began to chat about living together in Melbourne. But I should have realised he wouldn't be the only person who was going to react that way.

•

Days passed with no further information, and I began to get stressed. The Bulldogs and the Giants couldn't agree on the trade terms, and time was running out. Liam gave me a running commentary of the negotiations, but his iMessage updates only came through sporadically.

One day, when I connected to the wi-fi, a text came through that sent shivers down my spine. It was from Leon Cameron. *Shit.* Reading through the message, my heart sank.

'G'day Tom,' he wrote. 'Tried calling, crazy few days. Looking forward to getting you back to the club and a big preseason.'

It was a disaster. *Has the deal fallen over?* I forwarded the message to Liam but he didn't respond.

There wasn't much time left in the trade period, and I had all but resigned myself to returning to the Giants. Getting home to Melbourne had been so close, and now I was devastated. *My life is ruined,* I thought.

But Liam was a seasoned deal-maker, and he hadn't given up hope. When I finally heard back from him, he told me that he was going to put some pressure on the Giants. 'I'm going to make them uncomfortable,' he wrote. 'I need to go and speak on your behalf in the media, and make it clear that there is no way you will stay beyond next year. Are you okay with that?'

I was ready to do anything to avoid going back to the Giants. 'Go ahead,' I messaged back.

'Tom hates living in Sydney,' he told the media soon after. 'He will be coming back to Victoria, no matter what.' He piled on, with statement after statement on my behalf, none of which I'd actually said. As I watched from a distance, the spotlight turned onto the Giants, and it looked like things were heading in the right direction. *Maybe . . .?*

But the last full day of the trade period came and went, and there was nothing. 'Both clubs have gone home for the night—no progress, mate,' Pickers wrote. We had until 2 p.m. the next day to file a trade.

I barely slept that night, and the next morning was groggy and exhausted. This was the day my dream was going to fail, I was sure of it. I prepared myself for disappointment. My friends got ready for another day on the water, searching for waves.

'You surfing?' Brevin asked.

'Nah,' I replied. I had to stay behind and see it through to the deadline. By midmorning, there was still no news and the boys still hadn't gone surfing as the wind wasn't quite right. I stared at my phone, watching the clock. Finally, it buzzed.

Here we go, I thought, feeling sick. *Here comes the bad news.*

Liam wrote just three words: 'It's done, mate.'

I was a Bulldogs player! I was going home! *My career starts again, right now.*

8

SCRUTINY

Flying back to Australia, I couldn't help but wonder if there would be press waiting for me at the airport. I had a vague sense of the gravity of what had happened, but it was hard to get a good read from so far away. My entire life had changed, and I was optimistic about the future. I felt genuine excitement for my football career again, something that I had missed during my season with the Giants—but in the meantime, there was much to do.

I had a lease in Sydney that I would have to break. I needed to get in contact with staff at the Bulldogs and the Giants to sort things through. I had to undo the entire move I had done a year earlier. Luckily, Dad was happy to help with the logistics of the move back home. We planned a trip to Sydney to pick up my furniture, clothes and other belongings, pile everything into a truck and haul it back to Ringwood, back to my parents' house.

I had received a few supportive messages from Giants players since the trade was announced, which I appreciated greatly. I hated feeling like I had offended people or seeming unappreciative of the help I'd received during my time with the club. But it was inevitable that there was going to be a backlash.

I sensed a swift change of attitude from most of my former teammates, and their criticism found its way to me through both newspapers and social media. *We were friends a month ago*, I thought. Jezza told one journalist that he would 'prefer a pig-shooter over a city slicker any day'—I was the city slicker, traded for a pig-shooter. That was funny, at least. Others were more direct. For the first time, I felt genuine animosity towards me from my old teammates, from the media and the football public.

I wasn't surprised at the stir the trade caused—mine was a record-breaking deal, and footy fans like to have an opinion about how clubs spend their money. But the nastiness shocked me. I felt like people couldn't see past the dollars—see that I was a nineteen-year-old who was just trying to find my way in football. I hadn't put that price on myself, but who in their right mind would turn down an offer like that?

It was hard to work out how much of the pushback I felt was real and how much was just me being paranoid. Certainly there was something there, but I repeated what

I heard and saw over and over again in my mind. I felt like I was at the epicentre of the football news cycle, and a lot of the commentary was negative. The overwhelming impression I had was that people didn't think I was worth it—that I could never achieve the heights required by this enormous contract. No matter what I did, I couldn't possibly be worth it.

Why do people dislike me so much? I wondered. *Why is this contract causing so much animosity?*

I felt as though people had changed their opinion of me overnight. Yesterday I was a promising young footballer; today I was an overpaid hack. I couldn't make sense of it. And hearing people who actually knew me pile on cut me even more deeply.

I knew that the only way to escape the lonely feeling I had was to immerse myself at the Bulldogs. I needed to begin my training and start this new chapter.

•

My commitments at my new club began shortly after I moved back to Melbourne. It was a scary but exciting time at the Western Bulldogs, with high hopes for the year ahead— but there was no coach or captain. Despite his assurances earlier in the year that he would be there for at least two more seasons, Brendan McCartney was gone, while the club captain, Griffen, had gone up to the Giants. I was the great hope for the Bulldogs' future and the football media wanted to talk to me about it.

Denis Bicer was the media manager at the club and I liked him immediately—he was sharp, supportive and excited about my future. 'Don't worry about the media, mate, I'll handle them,' he told me. That gave me some comfort, though I was unsure exactly what he meant. He told me that my first media engagement—the very first thing I would do as a Bulldogs player—would be to attend a skills clinic at Williamstown North Primary School. 'It's a good, friendly environment, and Nathan Hrovat will be there as well,' Denis explained.

I had played at Vic Metro with Nathan, who I knew fondly as 'Rat', and I loved his energy. That was comforting too. I expected that my interactions with the media wouldn't be as easy as they once had been, and I was thankful to have someone I knew by my side.

The session consisted of a few drills with the kids, nothing particularly difficult. I was wearing a Bulldogs polo shirt, and it felt good to have my career at the club underway. When we finished up with the kids, I braced myself for the media onslaught. I had always been confident in front of journalists, but today I was nervous. I mustered a smile and stepped up to the microphones.

The questions started slowly. Mark Stevens asked about my experience of the trade, and someone else asked if I knew the Western Bulldogs' club song. 'Not yet!' I blushed. Quickly, the conversation took on a more serious tone.

'When did you sit down with the Giants and tell them you wanted to leave?'

'What didn't you enjoy about the club?'

'Did you play too heavy last year?'

'Are you amused or amazed by the amount of things going on at the Western Bulldogs at the moment?'

There was an urgency to the press conference that I had never experienced before. People were eager to ask me questions, and before I could even finish my answers, the next question was put to me. I did my best to be even-handed and diplomatic, and not burn any more bridges. *I didn't leave because of my teammates*, I thought. *Why are they asking me who the Bulldogs' coach is going to be? Why are they asking me if the Giants can retain their players?*

Surely no one cared what I thought about the AFL industry, I told myself. I didn't want to talk about the future of the football club—all I wanted to do was train and play. But it was clear that people saw me differently now, not only as a footballer but as a person. I wasn't a promising young teenager anymore, I was the 'seven-million-dollar man'. It was so uncomfortable. I didn't feel any different. I began to worry what my new teammates would think of me.

•

A couple of days passed and I began to settle into a familiar routine. I trained, lifted weights, saw my friends and relaxed at my family home in Ringwood. I had a few more media commitments lined up, which I wasn't looking forward to, but I sensed that the extra obligation came along with my new contract. And all the headlines about me had made me a target.

Since I'd arrived back in Melbourne, old friends had been contacting me. Some just wanted to reconnect, but others wanted to talk to me about investment opportunities. One Tuesday evening, I was sitting in a cafe in Richmond listening to a proposal about supporting young footballers. I was interested, but pain was building up in my back. I had experienced back spasms occasionally since I was about fifteen, so the sensation was familiar, though this one felt particularly painful. I suffered through it for an hour or so before I got home, took a Voltaren and went to bed. I had a 7 a.m. interview on Triple M to look forward to.

I needed to sleep, but the night was a restless agony of tossing and turning, cold sweats and spasms down my spine. I barely slept a wink. The interview the next morning was more of the same, full of challenging questions and things that I'd never been asked about before. In all these media spots I detected an undertone of resentment, and I became more uncomfortable with each interview that went by. *What did I ever do to you?* I wondered, wincing.

When I'd finished with Triple M, I went back to bed to try to sleep off the pain. I woke hours later when Mum came to check on me.

'What time is it?' I asked groggily.

'It's four-thirty,' she said. 'I just got home from work. Are you okay? You look terrible.'

I had never had back pain like this before, and it wasn't getting any better. In fact, it seemed to be worsening. Mum called the local GP clinic to make me an appointment, with any doctor they had available. The pain was unbearable by the time we arrived. The doctor told me that there was most likely something going on with my appendix. 'You need to take him to hospital,' he told Mum. 'There's no way of knowing right now what this is, but if it's his appendix and it bursts, it's going to be bad.'

We called Jake Landsberger, the Bulldogs doctor, to let him know the situation. 'Drive him to the Epworth right now, and leave the rest to me,' he said.

Within a couple of hours, I was talking to a surgeon, who informed me that almost certainly the problem was my appendix, and it would need to come out. 'There are no operating rooms here until tomorrow midday and it has to come out now,' the surgeon said. 'So we're going to Melbourne Private.'

I was discharged and we rushed across town to an empty and dark hospital, which seemed like it had been opened just for me. It was past midnight and things moved quickly—I was soon in an operating room, and an hour later I was appendix-free.

I was discharged the next day. That night, my phone began to buzz repeatedly as messages flooded in. *What's going on?*

I wondered, jumping online. I found it almost instantly—an article had been published by the *Herald Sun* with the headline 'Football's Most Expensive Appendix'.

I was astounded. *Is this for real? What the hell has my appendix got to do with my contract?* I'd been trying to grapple with how much things had changed, but the penny dropped when I read that headline. I wasn't Tom Boyd the person anymore. I was Tom Boyd the footballer. Everything that was happening in my life was suddenly wildly interesting to the wider public, including my appendix.

I disliked the direction things were headed, and the change I sensed in my own attitude. I had always been open with the media, but now I wanted to hide from them.

•

My recovery would take two weeks, which would see me through to the beginning of preseason. With no running or weights allowed, I was exempt from the first training sessions, which was a relief. I'd always found the first day of a preseason stressful, and now I had a genuine excuse to avoid it. But soon a panic came over me as I realised that not being at training was going to make it more difficult for me to prove myself to the team. For my entire football career, I had been taught to earn my stripes by putting my head down and training hard. Now there was no way I could do that. I worried my way through the final week or two of the off-season before my first day of training arrived.

Walking into Whitten Oval was like going back in time. The ground was filled with AFL legends, the names and faces of champions lining the walls. It was such a stark contrast with the Giants' brand new facilities in western Sydney. After playing for a club with no history, it was startling to walk into one that was rich with it.

It was daunting, too, to be the new kid again, having to learn new faces, names and personalities. The structure and obligations would be different here, and I didn't know what to expect. I wanted nothing more than to turn up and get stuck into training. I had hoped the routines of a preseason would help me adapt to the unfamiliar environment, but the reality was vastly different. I was unfit, unable to train and completely separated from the team, who didn't know me at all.

For the next few weeks, I watched from a distance. I swam in the pool, ran laps of the oval and did an array of exercises in the gym. I tried to be patient, to complete my limited program as best I could, but I had the distinct feeling that I was falling behind.

•

The commute from Ringwood to Footscray was killing me. I had to drive from one side of Melbourne to the other every day, and the traffic was insane. Sitting in my Subaru made my back ache and sucked the energy right out of me. I realised also that I had outgrown my parents' house in the year I had been away. Mum was getting on my nerves, always giving me jobs to do. 'I'll do it later,' I'd tell her, brushing her off. I'd grown accustomed to setting my own schedule and not having to answer to anyone. What I needed was a place of my own, somewhere closer to the club.

Brevin and his wife-to-be, Lara, had invited me to hang out at their house in Footscray whenever I had to train. 'If you ever need a place to crash, just let me know,' Brevin had offered kindly. It was a good interim measure, I thought. I was a grown-up, and although Brevin's spare mattress felt like it was made of concrete, it was better than being back at my parents' place.

Nick Vlastuin and I had decided to share a place together and were searching for somewhere to rent, but in the meantime, on nights when I had late finishes and early starts, I would stay at Brevin and Lara's. Their company was amazing—and it was brilliant having friends outside of football. I loved being able to switch off, come home and spend time with 'normal' people, even if it was only temporary. Nick and I found our own place in South Yarra not long afterwards.

Meanwhile, my preseason training was completely different to anything I had done before. We still didn't have a coach, for starters, so the team was being managed by our high performance manager, Justin Cordy. The assistant coaches ran the football components, but for the most part 'JC' was in charge. And he was big on fitness. He was firm but fair, and supportive of me.

After weeks of avoiding it, I was eventually cornered to do my skinfolds, which was a horrible prospect. I hadn't been training much since my appendix surgery, the outcome was inevitable. 'Not good enough, Tom, this needs to come down,' JC told me.

I was embarrassed, as always. Every time I went through the process, I couldn't help but be disappointed in myself. I would think back to every little thing I had eaten, every sugary drink I'd consumed, and feel incredibly guilty. Justin and the head physio, Chris Bell, sat down with me and outlined a plan for me to return to football training after Christmas. Until then, I would work on my fitness, my strength and all the little things that I needed to improve on. 'It's a long year, mate. We need to give you a good base to work off,' they told me.

They were patient, but every day I spent on the sidelines took its toll. I felt frustrated and alienated from my teammates. *I would be able to connect with them if I was out there.* I wanted to prove my worth, but I couldn't. I was sure they were all wondering why I was being paid so much.

As the weeks progressed, the Bulldogs were getting closer to signing a new head coach. Dad and I had been chatting about who it might be, but I hadn't worried about it too much. 'Imagine if it's Peter Sumich!' Dad said. The former Eagles great was in the conversation. 'For the first time in your career, you'll have a tall bloke as a coach!'

We laughed about that—my junior career had been plagued by short coaches, including Dad, who always considered himself a 'Collingwood six-footer'. I had caught him for height at age fourteen, and I knew he was really more like five-foot-eleven (with shoes on).

Luke Beveridge was eventually named the new Bulldogs coach. I didn't know anything about him, but my uncertainty was washed away during our first meeting. He was warm, friendly and clearly smart. He wasn't in a rush, but rather excited to explore what we could do as a team, and what I could do.

'Tom, there's only a handful of players in the competition who can be relied on for contested marking every week, that's what we want from you,' he said. 'At this stage, I don't want you to ruck—we'll focus on your forward play.'

I was filled with hope, which felt amazing. I was a central part of the new coach's plans, not just part of the squad. I hadn't felt this way at the Giants, because there were so many talented key position players, but 'Bevo' made it clear that the key forward spot on this team was mine to lose. I had an incredible amount of work to do, and I needed to improve—a lot—but I left that meeting feeling inspired.

A new program was tailored for me straightaway. I told them I was concerned about how heavy I had been during preseason at the Giants, that I wanted to be able to run better and be lighter. The high performance staff agreed. Instead of weights, I would do cross-training with Jack Redpath and Stuart Crameri, gruelling cardio sessions to help with my fitness. My training sessions were all about running, pounding the road outside the oval, trying to catch Tom Campbell, a ruckman with extraordinary endurance for someone of his size. Tom broke me, every time. I was left labouring behind, struggling to keep up with him, trying my absolute hardest.

My diet was strict, set by the club to help me drop weight: low-carb, low-calorie. I struggled for energy during my main training sessions, so I would break the diet and have some Weetbix before those big days. As difficult as the training was, I felt support for my development that was specific to my needs, and I was improving every day.

Bevo was different from what I was used to: his emphasis was on improving our football ability. We did increasing amounts of match simulation, and focused on skill more than I had ever done before. 'You need to learn how to play this style of football together,' he told us.

It was a style completely different to anything I'd seen. We would attack from defence, take risks, move fast. It was exciting, and the squad was taking to it rapidly. I had a growing sense of hope. *This is the best team I have ever played with*, I thought. I'd had the same thought the year before, but this was different: the Bulldogs were more than a group of talented, competitive individuals. We were a team.

•

A year earlier, I had thought that the good players didn't need preseason games. I had always imagined that the stars coasted through, making sure they didn't get injured. I asked one of my teammates at the Giants, Adam Tomlinson, if he hated preseason games, and he had replied, 'Nah, preseason games are great. You're as fit as you ever will be, not sore. It sets you up for the year, gets you into form.' That conversation had completely changed my perspective. In juniors, it had always been a time to coast through, and often I didn't play or played only limited game time. But AFL football was different, and with my first Bulldogs preseason games approaching, I was eager to impress.

Our first outing was hosted at our home ground, Whitten Oval, and it was against Richmond, including my house-mate, Nick. It didn't feel like my first real game for the club—it was only a practice game—but still I was incred-ibly nervous. Whitten Oval was notorious for the wild, windy conditions it often had. The game was a scrappy affair and I was quiet—I received a downfield free kick to score a goal, but otherwise didn't contribute much. I was disap-pointed but also knew that I had time up my sleeve; after all, I was certain I was going to play in Round 1.

I missed the following week's practice match due to a back issue, but came back for our final preseason game, against Collingwood at Docklands. 'This is a full dress rehearsal,'

Bevo told us in the lead-in. 'We're going to pick the Round 1 players from the team that is selected today, so give it everything.'

I was in full match mode. I was conscious that I hadn't yet earned my spot for Round 1. *I need to show something.* I couldn't bear the thought of my teammates talking about me behind my back, saying that I didn't deserve my spot on the side—or, worse, that I was being favoured. I was determined to win my spot in this team.

I showed improvement. I covered more ground and took some marks; I even kicked a nice snap goal, surprising myself. As the game wore on, I felt more and more confident.

Towards the end of the third quarter, I marked strongly on the lead but my opponent, Nathan Brown, landed clumsily on my legs, giving me a horrendous cork in my calf. My mind went back to a couple of years earlier, when I'd missed three or four weeks with a similar injury. *Oh no.* I limped off for a check-up but made it back out, saw out the game and celebrated a convincing team win.

•

We were in the best possible shape as a club leading into our Round 1 match with West Coast. Our midfield had been dominant during the preseason matches, led by Marcus Bontempelli, my teammate in my Vic Metro days. Marcus had dazzled everyone in the three preseason fixtures, following on from an incredible first year in 2014. I felt a ping of jealousy: *How good would it be to play that well?* But I shoved that thought out of my mind as our season started. Marcus worked too hard and he was too nice for my jealousy.

With Round 1 just around the corner, all signs pointed to me playing my first AFL game for the Bulldogs, but the signs did nothing to calm my uncertainty as the day drew closer. I still had so many doubts about my ability at the top level. I wasn't sure what was an acceptable level of performance, given my contract status. I wanted to blend in with my teammates, but I wanted to stand out as well.

Early in game week, I received the news that calmed my nerves. 'You're playing this week, Tom,' Bevo told me. 'Congratulations.'

My jumper was presented to me by a member of the Bulldogs fraternity, Ron Stockman, who had worn the number 17 in the 1954 VFL Premiership side. Ron spoke about how much the game had changed since his time, how much the job had changed and, of course, how much the pay had changed. 'When I played, we used to play for a couple of bob a week! Now I hear that some kid is being paid a million dollars a year!' he laughed.

I was horrified. *Does he know that kid is me?* Was I ever going to be able to get away from this constant conversation about my salary?

Ron then spoke about making the best of our time, putting our heart into the game. Then he called me up to the front and shook my hand. 'Wear this number with pride and kick more goals than me—I only kicked one!' he smiled.

I felt humbled and kept my comments brief. 'Thanks, Ron, for presenting me with this jumper. I hope I can wear it proudly. I'm really just looking forward to getting out there with you boys on the weekend.'

I was embraced by my teammates and my embarrassment subsided. All I wanted was for people to forget about me. What mattered was winning a game of football on the weekend against West Coast. As Bevo told us, 'Round 1 is only worth four points, but it always feels like it's worth a lot more to start your year off on the right foot.'

West Coast looked a tough opponent. They had stars across their lineup and it was going to be a real test. I would be defended by Jeremy McGovern, but I knew he'd have plenty of support.

The game was a tight affair. An early mark on the lead went straight through my fingers, and the crowd roared in laughter and disappointment. *Not a good start*, I thought. I ground away as the quarters went by, quite anxious to score, because I knew that was what people expected of me, but I couldn't get away from the Eagles defenders.

As the last quarter began, there was only a goal between the two teams, and the importance of starting the season with a win was the only thing on our minds. Bob Murphy, our captain, received a handball, took a bounce and kicked long to me. *Yes!* I marked strongly. The angle was tight, but

I was only 25 metres from goal. My routine kicked in. I went back and nailed it. I turned to the crowd, I felt the roar and celebrated with them—*C'mon!* I was filled with joy as my teammates surrounded me. And the goal meant something— we were back in front. From there we kicked away, running out victors by ten points.

As we sang the team song, I was showered with Gatorade. I had officially won my first game as a Bulldog, and relief, joy and pure excitement came over me in the afterglow. My proud parents hugged me despite the sticky sports drink on my skin. I felt incredible.

After getting home, I calmed myself down. *This is only the start*, I thought. *I need to improve again next week.* I couldn't afford to linger in the moment. There was a long season ahead.

•

Before I knew it, the weeks were rolling by. Better games against Hawthorn, Adelaide and Sydney were balanced out by goalless games, and dragged down even further by a Round 8 game against Melbourne, where I had only one disposal and was subbed out of the game. The reviews were brutal. Comments surfaced of Bob Murphy sledging Melbourne's key forward Jesse Hogan. 'You can't miss those! You are your team's great hope!' Murph was reported to say.

Hogan supposedly turned around, pointed to me in my red vest on the sidelines and said, 'There's your great hope.'

The scrutiny I was under was brutal. When my performances improved and I played well, people said, 'Well, so he should—that's what he's paid for!' And when I played poorly, it was a devastating spiral of criticism and vitriol: 'Waste of money!' 'Overpaid!' 'Reckless contract offer!'

My mood followed the trend of my performances. When I played well, I would feel relief, a sense of freedom in my daily life. When I played poorly, I felt ashamed to even show my face in public. I was embarrassed to talk to my friends, and terrified of receiving abuse on the street. No matter what those people close to me advised—that I had to be patient, that I was only young, that 'Tom Hawkins didn't get there until year five'—nothing seemed to change the way I felt. In my mind, when I played badly, I was a bad person who was disappointing everyone.

I was having difficulty sleeping again, and a bad game only it made worse. I would replay mistakes in my mind, and worry obsessively about the prospect of failure as the next game approached. I spent endless hours in the middle of the night tossing and turning, staring at the ceiling, willing my mind to stop churning, desperate to sleep. But it only got worse. I went to sleep tired and woke up exhausted, and my exhaustion began to drag down my motivation.

As the season went on, I had good games and bad ones, but I was spiralling. I began to struggle, just like I had the year before, to remember why I was playing football. My constant worries about my performance, about what people were saying, about what they thought of me, about failing, meant that the enjoyment was being sucked out of the game, yet again.

I tried to find a spark that would ignite me to have a positive second half of the year. I was hoping our game against Brisbane in Round 12 would be exactly that—Dan McStay was playing for Brisbane, so it would be the two of us, best mates from way back, knocking around on the football field together. I had been looking forward to it for a while.

Perhaps because of that positivity, in the game things just clicked. Dan was playing well for Brisbane and I was playing well for the Bulldogs, so it was like a childhood dream come true. Our friends were in the stands watching and cheering, along with one of our teachers from school, and for a second it almost felt like I was back playing for Eastern Ranges.

We came out winners and I finished the game with four goals, a career high, though I was slightly disappointed that I had missed an easy opportunity late in the game. I should have been ecstatic—it was probably my best game of AFL football to date—but I didn't feel ecstatic. I didn't feel much at all, just a quiet sense of relief that I wouldn't be the focus of everyone's criticism that week. *I hope.*

Daniel Giansiracusa congratulated me after the game. 'Gia' was so passionate about helping me improve and had done a lot of work with me. 'I wish you'd have kicked that last one, that would have really driven it home for me,' he said.

I was chuffed—he was a hard man to get praise out of, and could be quite confronting at times.

Denis Bicer caught up with me after the game as well. He had proven to be a fierce defender of me as a player, showing no hesitation in protecting me from what he deemed unwarranted or unnecessary criticism. His energy was electric, and he was greatly loved around the football club. I really appreciated him.

He greeted me with his characteristic huge smile and hug. 'Well done, mate!' he enthused. I thanked him and we laughed, and he pulled me in closer. 'Just watch, you'll get the rising star nomination this week, trust me!'

I didn't know what to say. *It's my second season*, I thought. *Am I even eligible?*

In the aftermath of the game, I tried to push that feeling of relief I had into satisfaction, even happiness. I wasn't happy, but my mind was more peaceful than it had been for some time, at least during the day. My nights were still filled with racing thoughts and doubts. My first goal had been a 'gimme' handball in the goal square from Jordan Roughead. I had dropped the ball, but narrowly avoided disaster by soccering it through. I replayed this moment over and over again in my mind until it almost felt like I had missed the goal.

On the Monday morning, I walked through Faulkner Park for a light recovery. It was just around the corner, and

Nick and I often went there to skate or walk Nick's dog, a 'Spanador' called Taz. My phone rang; it was Denis. 'You're this week's rising star, mate! Congrats! I told you so!'

Again, it wasn't so much joy that I felt but a sense of relief. I had dreaded the thought of being nominated as a rising star more than I had looked forward to the prestige of being recognised in this way. I was simply glad to not miss out.

Denis continued, 'I know you haven't done much media this year, but we are going to need you to do a presser for the AFL as part of the nomination. I'll be right next to you and make sure they don't harass you too much.'

I appreciated Denis's support, but I felt confident in front of the media. In a way, I was more comfortable dealing with them directly than I was with seeing and reading what they said about me. It's much harder for people to be cruel to your face.

The press conference the next day was the first time I'd faced the media as a Bulldogs player, more or less. The questions were mostly as I anticipated.

'How does this nomination make you feel?'

'Is this a reward for effort after the ups and downs of your career?'

'How have you seen the first half of your season?'

'Do you feel the scrutiny on you is warranted?'

Having been sheltered from the media by the Bulldogs, they almost now seemed like the enemy. I was running on autopilot. I didn't want to show them any vulnerability, for fear they would exploit it in one way or another. I didn't feel comfortable sharing who I really was. I had been trained to give clichéd answers that didn't lend themselves to headlines, and I had mastered the party line: 'It's not about me, it's about winning each week.' I told them I was trying to work on the non-negotiables in my game, competing in the air and bringing the ball to ground, but really these were empty expressions.

I doubt the journalists found my statements worth their while. Really, I could have sent them some pre-recorded lines. I knew that I couldn't avoid the scrutiny, that the great opportunities in my life had come with the condition that people were going to criticise or analyse my every move. But it was beginning to wear me down. I simply wasn't enjoying football like I used to, and football was my entire life. Joy, for me, had simply become relief from fear. And my failures weighed me down heavier than they ever had before.

•

The following week we played St Kilda and we won again, but a fumble early in the game had cost me a shot on goal, while an awkward tackle had sent pain shooting through my knee. I had played out the game but I woke the following morning virtually unable to walk. A scan at Victoria House Medical Centre followed.

After being swarmed by press outside the medical centre, I was told that I had a grade one medial ligament strain in my knee. Our physio Chris Bell explained the injury to me: 'Often the lower-grade strains are more painful, but your knee is stable, so we'll see how we go this week.'

But running, let alone training, proved unbearable. I couldn't kick, turn or run at any decent pace without agony in my knee, and I was ruled out of playing the following round. I hoped the pain would improve over the weekend, but it refused to settle down. I managed to do some running, but I wasn't even able to finish my swimming sessions without assistance, the pain from kicking was so severe. *There's no chance I'm going to be able to play in Cairns this week*, I thought.

Things off the field weren't improving either. My regular lack of sleep meant I was struggling to cope with the rigours of training. I was shattered most of the time, and felt I had lost all my power and explosiveness. The quality of my training results was falling away, and I had the overwhelming sense that whatever goodwill the game against Brisbane had bought me was rapidly diminishing. After a quiet game against St Kilda and a week off injured, I was out of form again. I knew that I needed to play well in my next game.

Although my knee was sore, I was told that I was expected to play against Gold Coast that weekend, which caught me off-guard. I hadn't trained for ten days and was struggling to complete even minor lateral movements or kick. But there were no excuses. I would be put through my paces at training on Thursday, and then deemed fit to play. I was filled with anxiety and doubt. If I played poorly, I had a horrible feeling that I would be dropped from the side.

Thursday's session did not go well. The injury was improving, but I was still incapable of kicking or changing direction without significant pain. At one point, I rolled around for a 25-metre kick on my right foot and the ball barely travelled five metres, the pain was so severe. I left the field to talk to the physios. 'I can't kick, I can't change direction—how am I supposed to play?' I was convinced that they would think better of it.

'There's no significant structural damage and you haven't had any pain relief while training,' they told me. 'We have a few days up our sleeves to settle it down. You'll be right.'

I didn't believe them. A sick feeling filled my stomach as I swallowed the news, as well as a strange kind of dissonance. This was the first time I was worried not about being overlooked, but about being selected to play.

We travelled to Cairns and started preparing for the game, but everything felt wrong. Along with my knee issue, I felt lethargic, drained, and was struggling to overcome my serious doubts that I could play. Along with the fear of playing poorly and being dropped, I felt like I was on the edge of the team—that my teammates were getting frustrated with me. In all likelihood, if I hadn't played well against Brisbane, I would already have been dropped to the reserves. I was holding on by my fingernails, and dragging them down.

The muggy Cairns weather added to my worries, and the pre-game warm-up confirmed my worst fears. As I went through my pre-game goalkicking routine, I realised I still couldn't do it properly. *I can't kick long set shots and I can't kick around the corner. How am I going to get through this game?* One of the worst things to have in your mind before a game of AFL football is doubt, but even worse is the fear that you are genuinely incapable of playing properly. *I shouldn't be out here.*

My fears were confirmed early in the game. I was slow, heavy, and the frustration from my teammates was evident. I was letting them down, playing terribly, and pretty soon I was dragged to the bench. A serve of genuine and deserved criticism came my way, and I tried to steel myself to provide a better contest. But I played terribly, and was terribly disappointed. We won, but it didn't matter—I might as well not have been out there. In fact, I sat on the bench for a large portion of the second half because I wasn't contributing to the game.

The crushing feeling of shame that hit me was the low point of my career to that time. *What is wrong with me?* I thought. I deserved to be dropped; in fact, I welcomed it. *Why would anyone pick me after that performance?* I wallowed in self-pity and despair, knowing that regardless of how the team had gone, I had let my teammates and coaches down.

I'd heard their frustration on the field, and I'd listened to the crowd confirm my own thoughts: 'Why the hell are you getting paid as much as you are?' I tried to put on a brave face, but sensed that my time in the AFL side was done, at least for now.

Following the Gold Coast game, my days were filled with a sense of impending doom. I was waiting for a tap on the shoulder from Bevo, to confirm my worst fears— but that tap on the shoulder never came. My individual reviews from the game weren't good, as I expected, but Gia caught me off-guard with the news that I would be playing in the next round.

'We need to see improvement down in Geelong this week, Tom,' he told me. 'We need some of that spark back from earlier in the year.'

Written on his desk, on a piece of tape, were these words: 'Never forget how hard the game is.' Gia had had an illustrious career that had spanned over 265 games with the Bulldogs, and the message on his desk was to remind him that things always looked easier from the coaches' box. I respected him greatly for this—I knew that every criticism he gave me came from a place of fairness. But it also made disappointing him feel so much worse.

With the news that I would be playing against Geelong, a flicker of hope went through me. I had always played well at Kardinia Park. I loved the size and shape of the ground. Maybe I could do better.

After a disappointing start to the game, I was shifted into the ruck to try to get me involved. I felt more freedom, as I wouldn't be measured solely by my goals or marks. I found some energy and tackled and competed, and by the end of the game I felt like I had at least contributed in a positive way. It was an improvement on the week before. Although we lost, my performance didn't feel as bad as some others I'd put in that year.

After spending a week being certain I would be playing VFL, I now held some hope that I could hang on. *Maybe I can play some more time in the ruck, mix it with some forward time*, I thought. But the conversation I had been dreading the week before came suddenly the next Tuesday afternoon.

Bevo pulled me aside and told me that I wouldn't be selected that week. 'We just aren't getting enough out of you up forward, Tommy,' he told me. 'I liked what I saw in the ruck, but I don't feel confident just rucking you for a full game.'

It wasn't a surprise, but it felt like a punch to the stomach all the same. *Why can't I ruck?* I wondered. *Anything would be better than going back to the VFL.* I began to realise the magnitude of the things that would follow me being dropped—the media scrutiny, the abuse from the crowd. I was filled with shame.

I called Dad to give him the bad news, and he was pragmatic, as usual. 'You haven't been performing well, mate. It was going to come at some stage,' he said.

'But I was better on the weekend!' I retorted, frustrated that he didn't seem to be on my side.

'You were better in the ruck, but they aren't picking you as a ruckman, are they?' Dad said.

The truth stung. I wanted someone to tell me I'd been hard done by, that what was happening was unfair and the world was against me. In reality, it was no one's fault. I had been given every opportunity to earn my spot, a luxury not afforded most other players, but that truth was hard to admit to myself. My shame and disappointment mixed with my insecurity, filling me with frustration—and my frustration occupied my mind throughout the night.

I barely left home after the Bulldogs announced that I would be dropped. I felt like an absolute failure, and no amount of reasoning would convince me otherwise. I was the million-dollar-a-year player who was playing in the VFL. Within two days of finding out my fate, I had to attend my first meeting with the reserves side to prepare for the upcoming game. Although I'd trained with many of the players in the room, I felt huge trepidation about joining their team. I worried about what they thought of me, and whether they would be happy to play alongside me. I wondered how they felt about me being dropped. I couldn't for a second accept that it was okay for me to be playing VFL, not on the contract I was on, but it was difficult to know how much of my impression of myself as a failure was real or imagined.

My first week of VFL football was brutal, a game at Piranha Park against the Coburg Lions. The ground was a notoriously difficult ground to play at, let alone win. My teammates tried to prepare me for the experience. 'Have you ever played at Coburg?' they asked. I hadn't. 'It's a terrible ground—bring your long stops.'

I wasn't looking forward to the game at all, though Ashley Hansen, our VFL coach, was optimistic. 'I know you'd prefer to be playing AFL, mate, and we would love that too, but we are thrilled to have you here. We know you'll play your guts out for us.'

I liked Ash. He had always been supportive of me and I wanted to play well for him, and I was glad, given the poor conditions, that I was able to play ruck as well as forward. But the game looked like a disaster for us from the get-go. Coburg kicked the opening goals, and after a brief response we were resoundingly beaten, by 48 points, in the worst game our VFL side had played for the year.

I could barely even think about the result. The only memory I had, singed into my mind, was the brutal abuse that I copped from the opposition and their supporters. Even our own supporters seemed to have turned on me. Of course, the press turned up in droves to capture it. I was slightly comforted by the fact that my teammates had defended me fiercely: they had stood their ground and fought, literally, against the abuse and antagonism that came my way.

But that feeling of comfort quickly gave way to one

of guilt. *Why should they have to worry about looking after me? Why can't I just play better so none of them have to deal with this shit? What happened to all those supporters who were happy to have me at the club four months ago?* I was still a second-year player, on a second-year wage, but I knew that didn't matter one bit because of the contract I had signed. I knew people wanted to help me, but no one could understand what I was going through—or so I thought. *No one has faced this before,* I told myself. *I'm literally the first player to be offered a contract like this.* That thinking only added to my sense of loneliness and isolation.

•

I received positive feedback from the coaches after my first game in the VFL, but I would play in the reserves again the following week. Another week came and went, with another decent performance (three goals), but still no promotion back to the AFL side. I began to recall the eerie feeling of being a forgotten member of the club, as I had been during my time at the Giants, except that I was playing far better overall this year. I was actually playing well—but so was the AFL side, so it was hard to break into it.

My weeks became more and more draining. Usually I was expected to play for the VFL side and then go and watch the AFL side play, so I rarely had a moment to myself over the weekend. This, coupled with the emotional exhaustion I was feeling, plus the lack of sleep and my growing bitterness towards football, began eroding any pleasure I felt from my social life. I started questioning, once again, whether I wanted to play football at all, but I quickly felt guilty for that too. *People would kill to have what I have*, I told myself.

I continued playing pretty well in the VFL side, and was often one the best players. I kicked goals regularly and it felt nice to contribute, but any positive feeling I had got swallowed up by the constant speculation in the media. They badgered the club about my return to the side: 'Is Tom going to play this week?' 'How about this week?' It seemed everyone was talking about me and my career, but no one was talking to me. I felt like I had no control, and my opinion didn't count.

With every good game I played in the VFL, and every AFL game I watched from the sidelines, my frustration grew. There was no indication that I was even close to a recall. I began to wish that players in my position would struggle, so that I could get another opportunity. *I'm playing good football—what more do I need to do?* My thoughts were so self-focused—it was all *me, me, me*. My insecurities and the outside pressure for me to be back in the side had changed how I thought about people, about my team.

I had never wished that other players would struggle before so that I might succeed. *Some of these guys are playing for another contract*, I scolded myself. *Some of them are your good mates—you see these people every single day.* Every selfish thought made me feel more like an asshole. I had completely changed my outlook on sport and the way teams work, without really being aware of it, and when I realised this it scared the shit out of me.

•

After four or five decent VFL games in a row, and with no recall to the AFL side on the horizon, I played my first really average game in the reserves. Immediately, I had the crushing realisation that my AFL year was over. I felt so far away from where I wanted to be that a place in my club's top side was almost out of sight.

With the AFL team going on an exciting run into the finals, I would play my final game of the year against Werribee in the VFL. I watched dismally from the stands as the Bulldogs narrowly missed out on a victory in an elimination final against the Adelaide Crows at the MCG. Wrestling with my own insecurities and copping criticism from the fans as I watched that game was the hardest thing I'd ever had to do. *I want my teammates to do well, I know I do*, I told myself. But I wanted to be out there so badly that my feelings were clouded by jealousy and bitterness.

More than anything else, I wanted my failure to be someone else's fault, but I could only blame myself—which I did, over and over again. I tortured myself with the idea, fixating on the times I had fallen short, unable to focus on what my teammates were going through. I walked down to the rooms under the MCG in the wake of the Bulldogs' loss to show my support, but the desperation on my teammates' faces was hard to swallow. I felt sad for them; they had missed out by inches. But a small, selfish part of me was glad the season was over and I could get away from football again.

My end-of-season reviews were rough. I was disappointed by how my season had finished, but I tried to reconcile it with the improvements I'd made since the previous year. I had played five more games in 2015, and kicked twice as many goals, which was at least an indication that I could play at the top level. It seemed like a step in the right direction.

My conversation with the Bulldogs coaches was a challenging one. I hadn't played an AFL game in a couple of months, but it felt like I hadn't played all year. They told me I had to improve my running ability, my competitiveness and ability to play in the ruck. Big improvements were expected of me overall in 2016. Honestly, it was much the same as the review I'd had with Leon the previous year.

All end-of-year reviews from coaches are harsh—they're meant to motivate you to improve. The medical staff took a vastly different tack with me, however. They sensed my frustration, and reminded me that I had only recently turned twenty. Patience was important, they said. 'It takes a while for big guys like you to develop as players.'

On the one hand, I was reminded that no matter what I was paid, I was still young and had time to improve. On the other hand, I was reminded every second of every day that I was being paid to be a superstar, and that my performance would be graded accordingly. Without success, I was a failure, overpaid and underperforming, end of story. No matter what anyone said, I realised, the world would not be patient with me. I had no time to waste in becoming the player I was supposed to be.

9

CONNECTION

With the 2015 season behind me, I couldn't wait to get away from Melbourne, football and the challenges that it had posed. I was headed back to Indonesia—to the same camp that I'd been at during trade season the year before. I was joined again by Brevin and Nick, as well as one of my new Bulldogs teammates, Daniel Pearce.

I still had the coaches' mandates ringing in my ears: I had to be fitter, lose weight and get myself into the best shape I'd ever been in. I knew I had to start immediately. I planned my diet carefully in Indonesia—I skipped the rice at every meal, sticking only to proteins. When I was hungry after a six-to-eight-hour surf day, I drank coffee or hydrolytes to suppress my appetite and get me through to the next meal.

In between surfs, or on slow days, Nick and I ran through the village in the searing heat, much to the confusion of the locals, and up into the jungle. Once we left the island coast behind and entered the jungle canvas, we hit a suffocating wall of humidity but continued on over little streams and bridges, dodging locals on motorbikes. Nick was always far leaner than me, but thankfully he wasn't much of a runner— at least, not off the footy field. So we were a good match for each other. When we ran out of breath, we turned back, dripping with sweat and desperate for water.

If I had to train, and I did, this was the best possible scenario. I spent all day in the Indonesian sun, surfing and diving. I was starving most of the time, so much that I often felt sick, but being in the water was the perfect distraction. After over a month in Indonesia, I came back with a good tan and a lean physique, satisfied with what I'd achieved.

But preseason was approaching fast, and it didn't take long for my insecurities to come creeping back. I was happy with how I looked and felt, but I knew it was only the numbers that mattered. Was I light enough? Was I fast enough? I wouldn't know until I knew.

•

During the year, I had started spending some time with a girl named Anna Von Moger. She had been my next-door neighbour in Anglesea since we were toddlers—her five older brothers were often on our property, or we were on theirs, due to the lack of fences. Anna and I had never been that close but that began changing after my return to Melbourne. We found we had a lot in common. There was something growing between us, but it moved very slowly, because my overriding obsession, for yet another off-season, was to improve my physique.

I'd skip breakfast every day and wait until I was really hungry, around midday, then I'd go to Faulkner Park to do my running sessions, and I wouldn't eat until later in the afternoon.

My strange new eating habits caught the attention of both Nick and Anna, who had differing reactions. 'Why are you just eating berries and yogurt?' Nick laughed. 'It's two o'clock—I've already had three meals!'

'Not everyone can get away with that,' I responded. Nick was naturally lean—his skinfolds must have been 35.

Anna was more concerned. 'Why are you skipping meals?' she asked. 'You know that's not healthy, right?'

I told her I needed to lose weight—that I wanted to be leaner and fitter.

'You can do that on a balanced diet. What you're doing isn't healthy or sustainable,' she replied.

It's working, isn't it? I thought begrudgingly. *What does she know, anyway?* I continued to train hard and skip meals until preseason started.

The first day back was terrifying, as always. I had done so much work, but my doubts persisted. *Have I done enough running? Have I done enough weights? What about that session*

I skipped? There was always some weakness or failing I could pick over in my mind.

But this time the feedback was good, and the club was happy. I was complimented on my physique immediately, and I ran a personal best in the maximal aerobic speed (or MAS) running test, though it was still one of the lower scores among my teammates. The first couple of days of preseason were generally positive, but during my physical screening my shoulder almost dislocated, and the tone of my conversation with the medical staff shifted dramatically.

'You can't train with your shoulder this loose, Tom,' they told me. 'We're going to have to make you non-contact for a while—you might even need surgery.'

Totally out of the question, I thought desperately. *This can't ruin my preseason—I have worked too hard.* My shoulder hadn't been an issue for the last eighteen months, I protested.

The medical staff sensed my impatience and devised a plan for me to dive fully into preseason, barring any contact work or tackling, until I had time to strengthen my shoulder muscles and stability. Still, I was set apart. For the second year in a row, I wasn't out there with my teammates doing full training. I could run with them and do light skills work, but my shoulder was taped so tightly that I couldn't mark the ball if it was above eye height. I was under strict instructions to protect it at all costs.

My days were filled with slow, controlled, tedious shoulder exercises—it was mind-numbing, but I was obsessed with fixing the issue, so I spent my days off doing extra reps to try to accelerate my return to training. It took about a month, but I was determined, and I slowly reintegrated with the team, more eager to prove myself than ever, and conscious that I had fallen behind.

In some ways, the approaching 2016 season felt like a fresh slate. The frustration I'd felt at the end of 2015 had washed away over the last couple of months, and I was eager to turn my newfound fitness into on-field form. There was a good feeling around the club this year, a strong sense of optimism and purpose. We had shown that we were capable of playing finals: now we were expecting to get there.

My own expectations were growing, too. I began to demand the ball more in match play. I felt the pressure to perform in every single session, and got frustrated when my teammates didn't kick me the ball or when they made mistakes. I knew my frustration stemmed from my fear of not meeting my own expectations, but it didn't matter: I needed to be more of a target, and a more reliable and more consistent performer. Having lost my spot in the side in 2015, I wasn't taking any chances. I was desperate to make sure I was in the team for Round 1. I felt the pressure of the media and supporters, all of them waiting to learn if the Bulldogs' star recruit would get a game.

I started feeling more confident than ever that I would perform well when I got my opportunity. Not long before the preseason games began, the team travelled to Ballarat for a community camp where we visited schools and local sides, and also trained as a group. The training session was designed to 'keep our legs ticking over' while we were away from Melbourne. It was a mixture of skills and running, and some light competitive work, and it was going fine—until suddenly it wasn't.

In a low-level drill I was tackled and dumped to the ground. I heard the sickening sound of bone grinding on bone. *My shoulder.* I had blown out the back of the joint again. I couldn't lift it and I was in agony.

Anger pulsed through me. I couldn't believe it. This was a light session—it should have been minimal contact. Now my season might be ruined by one overzealous tackle. *This can't be happening. How the hell does this happen?*

•

My shoulder had been shoved back into its socket, and I waited to hear the bad news from the physio. I was adamant that I wasn't going to have surgery—that I needed to play the season and prove myself—but I also knew this couldn't keep happening.

Chris Bell sat me down for a sombre conversation about the next steps. 'You'll need to get an X-ray and an MRI, just to make sure you haven't cracked anything, then we'll make the call.'

'Am I going to be able to play?' I asked.

It was all I wanted to know. I was worried—I had never hurt my shoulder this badly before, and it was more painful than ever.

Chris shrugged. 'You're going to need to get this fixed at some point, mate. Whether that's now or at the end of the season, it's too early to tell.'

Thankfully, the X-ray gave us some positive news: there was nothing too serious going on. The MRI showed extensive posterior damage and something called a 'reverse haggle'. I sat down with Chris again and was thrown into a conversation that I wasn't ready for, and certainly didn't expect.

'You're young, Tom, and you're obviously an important part of the club's future, so you have a choice to make,' he said matter-of-factly. 'We are going to send you to a surgeon to get an assessment. If the surgery goes ahead, it's season over for you. It will take five or six months for your shoulder to return to full strength.'

My heart sank.

'The alternative is that we take a really extensive and cautious rehabilitation strategy to try to get your shoulder as strong as possible. We can definitely do that, but I've got to be honest, this is going to happen again.'

I barely paused before I responded: 'There's no way I'm getting surgery.'

Chris nodded. 'It is a choice and it's up to you,' he said. 'I'd still like you to go and see the surgeon.'

I shook my head. 'No way.' My experience seeing a surgeon when I was at the Giants had left me traumatised. I had walked in thinking I was fine, then been told I needed surgery, only to have that refuted twenty minutes later. I wasn't going through that again.

I rang Dad later, as I always did when I was uncertain about things, and told him what had happened.

'Bugger, mate, that's no good,' he responded. 'I understand why you wouldn't want to see the surgeon. After all, if there is one thing that surgeons know how to do, it's surge!' he chuckled to himself.

I didn't see the humour—I was too busy picturing myself in the stands with my arm in a sling.

Ultimately, the club accepted my decision and we set about planning out the coming weeks and months to give me the best possible chance of getting through the season ahead. My new strength routine involved tiny dumbbells, TheraBands and slow, mundane exercises. I had a program that needed to be completed every day, and I was diligent. I thought about nothing but improving my shoulder strength so I could get back to playing.

It was the second setback I had experienced in only a couple of months, and the lack of continuity in my training was frustrating me. Every session I watched from the sidelines was a missed opportunity to work on becoming a better forward and goalkicker, and to bond with my teammates. I was earmarked to get back out on the field by the second week of the preseason competition, and I was hellbent on achieving that. The prospect of missing Round 1 terrified me. *If I miss it, who knows when I'll get back?*

My training load ramped up gradually, and once again I became frustrated. I was in a rush to perform well in our scratch matches but I couldn't get things to click. *I'm running to the right places, I'm wide open—why am I not getting the ball?* I had convinced myself previously that, as a forward, it was hard to deliver a good game in the preseason. The games were scrappy, the skill level was low and there wasn't yet much synergy between the players. But I didn't want to settle for that.

Eventually, things clicked. In one of my first full training sessions, I wore a pink bib to signify that I was coming back from injury so I was 'non-contact'. What this meant really was: 'You can tackle him, just be aware.' Things couldn't have gone more smoothly. It was my best training session by far for the Bulldogs—I marked everything, found space and looked like one of the best players on the team for the first time in my AFL career.

The defenders playing on me claimed the pink bib was the source of my success, and this would be a running joke for months. 'If you can't get a kick, throw the pink bib on, Boydie!' It always made me laugh because it was connected to a happy memory. Pink bib or not, I finally felt like I had arrived.

•

The opening two games of the 2016 season were victories. I did okay against Fremantle and played well against St Kilda, pinch-hitting in the ruck and playing forward. I found my feet much quicker than I had the year before. I excelled thanks to my newfound fitness. A year earlier, I had spent much of my time on the ground sucking in the air, exhausted. Now I was able to cover more ground.

I felt like I belonged on the field, which was a very big change. I had put everything in my life on hold to focus on football, so it felt good to see the improvement. Still, the fog of disappointment seemed to follow me. Being fit wasn't enough—the Bulldogs wanted a seven-million-dollar champion. I struggled to blank my mind to the negative commentary that surrounded me, and I became increasingly obsessive about every little mistake I made during a game, labouring over them rather than focusing on what I'd done well.

Round 3 was more challenging, but I kicked my first and only goal late in the fourth quarter to put us ahead of Hawthorn by a couple of points. I sensed this might be my first really big moment in the AFL—my first time as a potential matchwinner. The moment passed quickly, as Hawthorn scored a goal up the other end.

The night went from bad to worse when we learned that Bob Murphy, our All-Australian captain, had done his ACL. The sourness in the rooms after the game was palpable, and it felt like things couldn't get worse, even though we'd shown great promise against the team that had won the last three Premierships.

The club was reeling, but we did our best to prepare for our next opponent, Carlton. We were favourites, going in. I wasn't playing well during the match: the old familiar fatigue was creeping in. A ruck contest late in the game saw me placed in an awkward position, and then *CRUNCH*—my shoulder dislocated again. I winced in agony but managed to complete another ruck contest with one arm before I ran from the ground, holding my shoulder in place.

My heart dropped as I sat on the bench and watched the remainder of the game. I was suffering more from the disappointment than from any pain. I had injured this shoulder three times now, and it was happening more easily and more frequently. I felt all my hard work slipping through my fingers.

The diagnosis was as I expected: bruising and tearing, the same issues as previously. I stressed to the physio that I had been doing everything I could to make sure it didn't happen; I had followed my program to the letter and stuck at it every day.

'These things happen, mate,' I was told. 'Your shoulder is very loose, but we are going to get it right. You've been through this a couple of times already—you know how to get it strong again.'

In a way, I was relieved. Knowing that I had a clear roadmap back to playing was comforting, but being on the outer due to injury worried me deeply.

•

The months leading up to my AFL return were challenging. My recovery was slow, but the pressure was mounting on me to perform. I had never felt pressure like that before, from all corners of the football world, including myself. Beyond any doubt, I was failing to live up to the expectations of the fans and the industry.

If I didn't force myself to focus, one day at a time, I felt like negativity would swallow me whole. My contract and the financial freedom attached to it came at the cost of feeling constantly trapped, like I was disappointing people, through some things that were in my control and others that were not. I internalised all my frustration and disappointment and tried my best to funnel it into my performance on the field, but the pressure was beginning to affect the way I lived my life. It didn't feel like it was firing me to improve; it was making me terrified of disappointing people further.

I couldn't find any solid ground internally: it was like I'd lost my direction and my ability to understand who I was as a person. I could only see my life through the lens of who I was as a footballer. The football club and my performance on-field dictated everything I was, who I spent time with, how I earned a living and how I valued myself. This fuelled a commitment to doing well, but with it came an unshakeable anxiety around how I was perceived.

I'd always been a perfectionist with regard to my football,

but this had been easier to manage when I was playing in the juniors. It had become harder and harder in the first two years of my professional career, but I'd never felt anything as intense as what I was feeling in 2016.

It was Round 17 by the time I made it back into the AFL side, and we were playing Gold Coast in Cairns. I hadn't played there since the year before, in a game that held terrible memories for me.

My stress in the lead-in to my return game was almost unbearable. I had given myself no option but to perform well. My sleep was interrupted every night, and I worked myself into a state as I prepared to play.

My teammates rallied around me as the game approached. I relished the support—they were now some of my best friends—but I knew they needed me to step up as well. They too had expectations of me as a player. I had to perform.

As the hours ticked by before the game, I told myself one thing to help me cope: *You don't have a choice.* I had to narrow my focus to just that moment, just that game, and get myself to the point where I could contribute to the team.

The game went well. I did my job and felt at home quickly—and with a win on the board, in hot and slippery conditions, I felt a thousand times better. I had tied myself in knots trying to prepare mentally for something that felt like Mount Everest, but turned out to be nothing more than a game of football. I welcomed both the exhaustion and the relief that followed.

The next week was a difficult one for the team. We had a devastating loss to St Kilda, and two major injuries: an ACL for Jack Redpath, and a horrific broken leg for my best friend at the club, Mitch Wallis. I played poorly that week, but I didn't care. Watching Mitch go through agony and despair in the days following the match gave me a great sense of perspective about what was real and important. It pulled me out of my own insecurities and introspective thinking, at least for a while.

I drove to the hospital after the game with Mitch's partner, Emily, and the scene there was genuinely distressing. He was in so much pain. I saw him again the next day, just before he had surgery, and was struck by the severity of his injury, the impact it was having on the people who cared about him, and the amount of work that was in front of him to return to football. I realised how lucky I was to not be in the hospital bed next to him, or in Jack Redpath's place in the next room.

I felt fortunate in that moment to be playing AFL. It was a feeling that I'd been without for a long time.

•

I settled into the AFL side over the weeks that followed. We were looking likely to play in the finals, and my sole focus was to be in the side when we got there. My form was good— being able to ruck as well as play forward meant that I wasn't relying on goalkicking alone to feel like I was contributing. As a team, though, we weren't tracking as well, as we were besieged by injuries.

Jack Macrae went down with a hamstring and Tom Liberatore with a sprained ankle during a game in Geelong. Three rounds later, it was our captain Easton Wood (standing in for Bob Murphy) who injured his ankle against Essendon. We were a certainty to play finals by then, three games clear of ninth position by the year's end, but we were barely a game outside the top four when we played our final home-and-away game against Fremantle. We were desperate to finish the regular season strong.

Our team was greatly diminished when we flew to Perth, with a number of brilliant players and team leaders nursing injuries at home. To add to the challenge, it would be Fremantle legend Mathew Pavlich's last match, game number 353. Although the Dockers were low on the ladder, they had plenty to play for.

From the opening bounce, things did not go well—we looked slow and a step behind. I led strongly into the forward line as the end of the first quarter approached and jumped to mark, but landed awkwardly on my ankle, which made a horrible crunching sound. I knew that sound, and I knew it wasn't good. The ankle had given me grief for years, ever since I'd injured it as a junior, on the same ground, in fact almost in the same spot.

I hobbled off the field and was taken straight down into the rooms, where the doctors looked it over. I was sure my day was done. 'How bad is it?' I asked, the pain only building.

'It's gonna be okay, mate,' the doctor told me. 'We'll look at it after the game, but for now we are going to give you something for the pain and get you back out there.'

I shouldn't have been surprised, but I was. I was certain that I needed to rest my ankle, especially with a final to play in ten days' time, but if the medical team gave me their blessing, I was determined to keep playing.

After a couple of jabs, some heavy taping and a few words of encouragement, I hobbled up the race for a fitness test just after quarter time. Chris Bell put me through my paces, and I jogged and jumped in front of the Fremantle supporters. 'You're shit, Boyd!' they hollered. I tried to smile through the pain as Chris called the coaching staff.

'He can't run more than seventy or eighty per cent, and he's struggling to jump and change direction,' I heard Chris say. 'What do you want to do with him?'

Hollered over the crowd noise, the response was abrupt: 'Put him in the ruck!'

So I set myself to play the rest of the game, with a sore ankle, against the biggest ruckman in the league, Aaron Sandilands, who had six inches and twenty kilograms on me. I managed to get through the game, even having some good moments, but as the painkillers wore off late in the game, the dull ache at the end of my leg turned into a searing pain.

We lost the match, but I didn't dwell on it—I was already thinking about the game ahead. Because of our loss to Freo, we would be returning to Perth to play West Coast, one of the top teams in the competition. We had slipped to seventh position on the home-and-away ladder, and our hopes of making a serious finals run seemed to have taken a massive hit. No AFL team had ever won the flag from seventh position.

•

I had played the last seven games of the regular season, and played reasonably well, but I still had a smattering of doubt leading into the first final. The review of our last game wasn't particularly good, and Bevo's brief lecture about how much we would need to improve if we hoped to progress in the finals left us all a little nervous. There were going to be significant changes to the team, he said. It would be a week or more before we found out who was playing, and I spent most of those days trying to quieten the voice in my head that said, *Maybe you didn't make it . . . maybe you're not good enough.*

There was a gradual, growing anticipation in the lead-up to our game in Perth. More fans attended each training session, giving their support (and advice), hoping that we could pull a rabbit out of the hat and snare a victory. I didn't have to wait long until I found out I was playing—a simple comment about the upcoming match-ups from Gia, the forwards coach, made me confident that I was in their plans. It's amazing the power that a throwaway comment from a coach can have on how you feel about your life.

I was going to play in my first AFL final! It was a proud moment and I was delighted to share it with my parents. I knew that it had been tough for them, watching me struggle through my football journey, and they were as eager as anyone to get over to Perth to witness me make my finals debut.

As the match day drew near, the coaches' plan for us started to become clear. A few of us made the trek to Perth a day early—me, Easton Wood, Jordan Roughead and Matthew Boyd, among others. We had all suffered from some swelling concern or another in the recent months and needed the extra time to recover after the travel.

There were ten or twelve of us in the advance party, and it was a great bonding opportunity. We trained together and got our minds set for the game, and it felt like a calm, focused preparation. The rest of the team got stuck at the airport in Melbourne after their flight was delayed, blowing out the light training session that was scheduled for that afternoon.

Those of us already in Perth waited patiently as the team's arrival time was pushed back over and over again, but my concern for them grew. Having your preparation completely thrown out before a game was tough, especially when a four-hour flight was involved. *Thank God I'm already over here,* I thought.

The team bus finally arrived at the hotel as the evening light was fading, with a bunch of weary and agitated players on board. It was too late to have our pre-game training session at the ground, so instead we headed to a nearby school, Trinity College, to do some stretching and a light skills session. It was 8 p.m. when we started, and three hours later for those still functioning on Melbourne time.

Against the odds, though, the group was filled with energy. Even though we struggled to see the balls whizzing around in the dark, it didn't feel like we'd been dealt a bad hand. This inconvenience only made us more determined.

•

Game day arrived, and I felt the best I had in a while; an extra-long break between games had me feeling fresh. I didn't often feel excited ahead of a game—usually I was consumed by nerves about my performance—but my fear of failure had been washed away by the only thought that matters in a final: *Win.* As the hours and minutes ticked down before the game, I felt more and more confident that we were a chance—that we could actually beat this team in front of their home crowd.

Bevo had the same sense. 'Why not us?' he asked us. We weren't looking ahead, but we all knew that if we won that night, we could do anything. As we walked up the race towards a hostile crowd, Bonti said something that sent shivers down my spine: 'Silence is golden.' We were ready.

After giving up two goals early in the game, we found our groove. We were sharp, connected and unstoppable. A thirteen-point lead at the first break turned into a 24-point lead at half time. But West Coast had a huge home crowd advantage, and we knew we couldn't allow them any thought of a comeback. 'Don't even give them a sniff!' Bevo told us.

And we didn't let up. When the final siren sounded, we were 47-point winners, shocking the rest of the competition.

I had played well enough, doing my job, as had everyone on the team, and the rooms after the game were ecstatic. We celebrated with each other, hugging and laughing, talking about the little mistakes and the perfect moments. Before long, the conversation turned to the following week.

'How far can we go?'

'No one can beat us if we play like that again.'

Bevo thanked everyone involved, not just the players, for what they had done to overcome the challenges of the past 24 hours and deliver a win. He told us to enjoy the moment. Over the next few days, other finals results would come through and we would start focusing on our opposition.

I had never felt the way I did after that game. I wasn't concerned about myself at all. I'd had a simple goal before the game, and we had achieved it—together. I didn't feel the need to critique myself as I had done after games for as long as I could remember. I felt like I could just sit in the moment, enjoy the win with my teammates and not think about anything other than the success we had achieved. It was a rare moment of peace.

•

Landing in Melbourne, it became apparent that we weren't the only ones excited by our elimination final victory. Fans and media greeted us in droves at the airport, and our supporters were smiling and cheering, decked out in Bulldogs paraphernalia. As tired as I was, it made me smile to see the joy that football brought to people. The excitement for our next game was starting to build.

We trained as normal, but the dozens of fans who had attended the week before had become a hundred or more. The atmosphere for training at Whitten Oval was more electric than it had ever been in my AFL career. For the first time, none of my fan interactions was negative—not a single one. Everyone who came along came with the sole purpose of supporting the team. They smiled, cheered and asked for photos. I wondered whether I had been imagining some of the vitriol I had received from Bulldogs supporters in the past, or whether these ones were just particularly nice.

It didn't matter for now. The club was buzzing with positive energy, and I felt more comfortable about being a footballer than I ever had. It had even changed the way I felt away from the football club. My days, once filled with stress and worry, were now marked by a warm, growing sense of anticipation. My nights were restless because I was excited, not because I was afraid. *Maybe football isn't so bad after all?*

Whatever was going on, I wanted it to last as long as possible.

•

The following week we were up against the premiers of the previous three seasons, Hawthorn. I barely noticed the chatter about the fact that we were underdogs—it didn't feel like that to me. Once again, in the lead-up to the game, I felt oblivious to the external noise around the game that had caused me so much anguish only months earlier. I wasn't worried about Hawthorn or their players, and I wasn't worried about my own performance—I just knew that we needed to win, and I believed we could.

Bevo told us we needed to be at our best, but also that we didn't need to change anything—that our core style was good enough, and we should just replicate the energy we'd brought the week before. Our usually arduous pre-game meetings were short and positive, and included a video of team highlights. 'This is our identity as a team,' Bevo told us. 'This is what it looks and feels like when we play our best.' It was a glorious collection of brilliant moments, a blueprint for success, and it gave all of us an incredible boost in confidence.

As the team's momentum was growing, the disparity between the haves and the have-nots was growing as well.

Those who were missing out because of injury or disappointing form had to deal with the great challenge of smiling through their heartache. Some knew they were missing what might be their only chance at AFL finals success.

I knew how that felt—I had been there the year before. I remembered the guilt and struggle I felt to be happy for my friends. There was nothing worse for me than feeling like I wanted others to fail because I was failing, but not everyone was wired like me.

Since breaking his leg, Mitch Wallis had been a magnificent support for me. He and I had become best friends after I joined the Bulldogs, and I was acutely aware that while I was feeling the best I ever had about football, he was trying to overcome one of the most horrific injuries that our sport could inflict. I knew he deserved to be playing in this semifinal far more than I did, but that wasn't the way things had turned out, and there wasn't a single thing either of us could do about it.

Mitch never complained. We spent most of our days together, either at the club or socialising away from it, and he had supported me through all the difficult moments I'd faced in recent times. Now the best support I could offer him was to distract him from the finals noise, so we spent the Thursday afternoon before the game watching a movie together.

'Thanks, mate, I needed that,' Mitch said.

I understood. Bob Murphy, Jack Redpath, Lin Jong, Mitch—these were all players whose luck had been worse than my own. There was no fairness to it. It was like there was this great elephant in the room, this glaring injustice as club champions and long-time players missed out on playing through no fault of their own. It was an unspoken reality of finals that I had never spent a huge amount of time thinking about—and that now I spent much of my time trying to ignore, for fear of losing the wave of positivity I was riding.

I had spent enough time smiling when I wasn't happy to know how exhausting that was, so I felt for the players who were watching on. But I had no choice but to keep moving forward.

•

The opening quarter against Hawthorn was a fierce one. We started well but were wasteful in front of goal, and we were down by a couple of goals at quarter time.

'It will click,' Bevo told us. 'We're almost there!'

He was sharp but not angry, intense but not aggressive, and he was right. The tide began to turn, and after a big second quarter we came into the long break a point down, but with the momentum clearly on our side. By the time the final siren sounded, we had proven ourselves. We had beaten the defending premiers by 23 points.

The week before had felt good, but something different had just happened. We had been down by as much as 23 points in the second quarter, but we hadn't given up.

It seemed like something special was growing in the team. I knew I could rely on every one of my teammates—that we would play and fight as one.

I had never been with a group that was so close. We were all very different as people, but as a team we were inseparable: we supported each other, cared for each other and played for each other. Whatever we had found over those last two weeks was special—players who had struggled at different points throughout the year had begun to play well again, and our usual stars were playing at their best.

I pinched myself as I looked up at the 88,000 people who had just watched us play. I'd dreamed about playing at a full MCG all my life. *I was in that crowd when I was a kid*, I thought, *and I'm one win away from playing here again, in an AFL Grand Final.* It was a thought that not long before would have been fanciful, but a shot at an AFL Premiership was genuinely only four quarters away.

•

The preliminary final was against my old side, Greater Western Sydney. I knew it was going to be hostile—there was so much history between us. After the buzz of the week before, it felt strange to think we would be leaving our fans behind, and that most of the people who had supported us through our training sessions and at the Hawthorn game would be watching from home.

I heard the first rumblings then of the preliminary final 'curse' that the Bulldogs fans had lived through—the club hadn't made it to a Grand Final since 1961—but it hardly seemed relevant to our team. We were young and on a roll, and the looming challenge of GWS was enough to worry about without adding a mystical curse.

During the week, I caught up with Emma Quayle, a footy journalist whom I liked and respected. I had met her during my junior football career and when I was at the AIS. We reminisced about times past and spoke about my journey from the Giants to the Bulldogs, and how, in a strange turn of events, these teams were now going head-to-head in one of the most important games in both clubs' histories. I was comfortable talking to Emma about most things, and even shared some of the challenges I'd had with my shoulder injury throughout the year.

The following day, I walked into the Bulldogs' training centre and was met by my coaches Joel Corey and Steven King, who approached me with concerned looks. 'Why did you tell Emma about your shoulder issues?' they asked.

I was genuinely confused. *What in the world are they talking about?* It turned out that in her article Emma had mentioned the injury and that I would need a reconstruction.

'They're going to target you now,' Kingy warned me.

I was bewildered. My shoulder injury was hardly a secret—I had spent months on the sideline after hurting it earlier in the year. *It's been taped up for every game! How can they not know?* I wondered. I was concerned for a while, but soon forgot about it and moved on with my week.

Walking out onto the ground at Spotless Stadium in western Sydney that weekend, two things occurred to me. First, it was brutally hot. Second, there were very few GWS fans. The stadium was blanketed in our colours, red, white and blue. It was an away game for us but it looked like our supporters outnumbered theirs by two to one, maybe even three to one.

As we warmed up, the Giants entered the stadium to an extraordinary response—they were viciously booed at their home final. I could feel the spirits of my teammates lift. Our supporters hadn't just come to match the opposition, they'd come to dominate them. It felt like it was our home game, and I felt invincible.

As it turned out, Kingy and Joel were right: even before the game had begun, Shane Mumford was smashing my shoulder, trying to put me off. Over and over again as the action started, the Giants' players whacked my shoulder, punched it or bumped me to make me uncomfortable. I gritted my teeth.

The game was ferocious, both in intensity and aggression, with neither side willing to back down. Years of animosity and overlapping history were poured into it. Two points separated us at quarter time. I was tired already and was struggling to get involved in the game, but the second quarter changed everything.

In a sickening clash, Zaine Cordy put a knee into the head of GWS captain Callan Ward, leaving him unconscious and unable to return to the field. Then my ruck partner Jordan Roughead had an eye injury, and he too was forced off and unable to return. The message came to me from the team's runner, Matt Inness: 'Roughy is off, Tom—you're our only ruckman.' I spent the remainder of the quarter rucking against the Giants duo of Shane Mumford and Rory Lobb, and came in at half time exhausted.

Roughy was in a bad way. His eye was completed clouded over with blood, and he couldn't see out of it. *Jesus, that looks bad*, I thought, but my concern for his wellbeing was quickly overtaken by the realisation that I was now our only ruck option. I would be expected to do the job solo against a seasoned and aggressive veteran in Mumford, who was notorious for his toughness. His ruck partner Lobb had six or seven centimetres in height and a significant reach advantage on me.

For whatever reason, though, I felt calm. I was determined—I had to do this, there was no other choice. If I failed, it was very likely my team would fail too.

I battled away through the third quarter, feeling like I was holding my own. I kept telling myself, *Just keep turning up, keep competing, don't drop your head*. I didn't have to play the next two quarters, I told myself—I just had to complete the next contest. I would take them one at a time, until the match was done.

I came to the bench for a short rest during the quarter and

Zaine Cordy went out as my backup ruck. He was shorter than me, and twenty kilograms lighter, and the Giants began to get on top of him. From the bench, I sensed the importance of the moment. The game was hanging in the balance. *I have to be out there*, I thought. *This is my responsibility.*

'Get me back on the ground,' I told the bench.

By the third-quarter siren, I was feeling overwhelmed by exhaustion. It was never-ending: *ruck, tackle, chase, follow up, ruck, tackle, chase* . . . I could feel my legs and my fast-twitch muscles beginning to slow. I was labouring between contests. All I wanted was to not be beaten—I had to make it a stalemate at worst.

It was one point the difference at the final break, and Bevo looked me in the eye, in front of the entire group, and said, 'Can you keep going? We need you out there.'

I told him I didn't need a break, that I could hang on for the final quarter. I had never felt more duty to my teammates. A powerful wave of determination came over me. I might not be the reason we won this game, but I had to make sure I wasn't the reason we lost.

Effort, after effort, after effort. The quarter grinded on, feeling like it was never going to end. I barely had the energy to celebrate the goals we kicked, or to acknowledge the goals we conceded. I just had to make it to the next contest—no excuses, nothing until it was over.

My teammates were inspiring—Marcus Bontempelli, Tom Liberatore, Jack Macrae, Toby McLean, Luke Dahlhaus,

Liam Picken—everyone encouraged me. 'Keep going! Next contest!' We had conceded the first two goals of the quarter, but clawed our way back in front, and then GWS evened the score with less than five minutes on the clock. Every contest that I was involved in felt like the most important moment of my career, and I was absolutely out on my legs. I was running on less than empty.

A late mark and goal by Jack put us up by five points, and we all took a deep breath. After a chaotic few moments, the Giants opened up the ground and looked all but certain to go down the other end and score, but a dropped mark let us back in, the ball skidding around. I got a handball and gave it to Jake Stringer, who centred the ball across the goals. Tory Dickson marked it, 25 out on not much of an angle.

How long is left? I wondered. *Have we done it?*

Tory took his time, running out the last few seconds. Before the ball touched his boot, the siren sounded.

We were going to the Grand Final.

•

Pure and utter exhaustion. I could barely lift my legs, my shoulder was bruised and battered, and I felt physically ill. I couldn't even summon happiness—I felt relief, mixed with an enormous sense of satisfaction. The whole team was exhausted, but proud.

We barely had time to process that moment, though,

before we were flying out of Sydney and our conversation turned to the next game. We would be up against the Sydney Swans. Would Roughy be able to play? Would there be any changes to our team? What was the week ahead going to be like? As well as everything had gone, we had a sense that things were unfinished. Our job wasn't yet done.

Kingy had been through a Grand Final week a couple of times before, and he said something that stuck with me: 'Whatever the result is next week, make sure you enjoy every moment of the week ahead. Soak it in—it's a week that you'll never forget.'

He was right—everything was different. Our entire schedule turned upside down, with additional media commitments early in the week, public appearances and the Grand Final Parade on Friday. It felt like a dream. I had been lucky enough to attend a few Grand Finals in my younger years, but couldn't fathom that I was about to play in one.

I thought back to those Grand Finals I'd seen, sitting way up in the top of the stands, looking down on the game from what felt like miles away. It wasn't the best way to watch a game, but it gave me such an extraordinary view of the crowd. In under a week's time, I would be standing in the centre circle, a 21-year-old footballer living out his childhood dream, looking up at some young kid up in the stands. I felt tingles down my spine.

After an incredibly slow Sunday, we were engulfed by media on Monday morning, every player on the team packed into the VFL change rooms with a huge cohort of journalists. In interview after interview, I answered some variation of the same handful of questions:

'How are you feeling?'

'How is your shoulder?'

'Are you ready to show your worth as a million-dollar player?'

After an intensely tiring hour, we left the tirade of questions behind. *Thank God that's over*, I thought. That was the last media call until Friday.

Outside the gates of Whitten Oval, Footscray was coming alive. Doors, gates and fences were painted in red, white and blue. Jason Sneddon, a great friend and the owner of the Railway Hotel in Yarraville, painted his pub in Bulldogs' colours. The noise on the periphery—the joy and excitement among our fans—was beautiful. I couldn't help but feel the growing momentum around the club. *Everyone wants us to win.* It felt like more support and love from the world than I'd ever had before.

Our training sessions were mobbed by fans, with thousands of people in attendance, cheering. It was incredible. As intensely focused as we all were on the task at hand, I had never smiled so much at footy training. On the track, everyone was in preservation mode as no one wanted to risk hurting themselves before the most important game of their lives. Every little ache or pain I had drew extra attention, and every glimmer of tightness or soreness was addressed with extra treatment and preparation.

As incredible as the feeling was overall, it was impossible to ignore the mental challenges that other people at our club were facing. Those of my teammates who were not guaranteed a spot in the Grand Final side were nervous wrecks for the first few days of the week. With a life-changing moment so close, it must have been torture to think it could all be taken away by a coach fiddling with the magnets on the team whiteboard.

Many players were injured or out of favour. Some had been integral parts of the team in times past. Others were great friends of mine. They had all worked just as hard as I had to get there. They all had their own stories. But they would not all get the chance to play in football's greatest game.

I had always heard the saying that it took a list of players to win a Grand Final, and I understood then how true it was. I felt real compassion for those who were left out, but I had to look forward as well. I had to continue riding the wave—to focus on the game ahead. I had no control over anyone else's situation; I was just lucky to be in the right place at the right time. The only thing I could do for my teammates was win, so I put my blinkers on and prepared for the match.

•

We had done everything we needed to do. We had recovered, trained, prepared—now all that was left to do was execute. After a normal Friday training, I would usually take it easy, relax at home, watch a movie, maybe catch up with friends or family. After training that Friday, I would be going to the Grand Final Parade.

We boarded the team bus (with a packed lunch in tow) and headed towards the MCG to join the estimated 180,000 people in attendance. An ocean of people was there to support the two teams before they went into battle the next day. It was surreal, but I followed Steven King's advice: I soaked it in and enjoyed the experience. *I may never have it again.*

Sitting in the back of a Toyota Hilux and being paraded through the streets of Richmond felt embarrassing, but it also gave me great insight to the vast number of people who love the AFL. I wondered what to do with my eyes, my hands. *Do I wave? Do I smile? What am I supposed to say to people?* My thoughts were racing. But before long I realised that all I could do was sit there and listen to voices from the crowd.

'Go Bulldogs!'

'Up the Swannies!'

'Million dollars a year? Get a kick, Boyd!'

'You're a hack, Boyd!'

'Toughen up, superstar!'

Even in that huge and generally loving crowd, the messages snuck through; my ear for some reason was more sensitive to the negatives. I had nowhere to hide, so I just smiled through it. *Just win, that's all that matters*, I told myself. I slept well that night.

The next morning, time seemed to move faster than usual. I gave myself extra time to get to the MCG as I knew there would be heavy traffic and multiple security checks to get through. I must have checked my bag fifteen times before I left the house to make sure I had what I needed, though it wasn't much.

A teammate of mine from GWS, Tim Golds, once told me something about preparing for a game that I lived by: 'Boots and mouthguard; everything else you can do without.' My mouthguard was always in the same place—my boots and spares too. (Later, when I got to the ground, I managed to get stuck in a queue of players' cars. I saw someone jump out the back of Tom Liberatore's car and I presumed he was just getting dropped at the ground, but I later learned that Tom had forgotten his boots! His friend was rushing back to his house to retrieve them.)

I had my music playlist set and ready on my phone; I had used the same one for the previous three finals games. I didn't have many superstitions, but it seemed silly to change it. I was ready.

The last conversation I had before I left was with Dad. We spoke on the phone, and the conversation was awkward, as he tried to contain his excitement and I tried to contain mine. After bumbling through a few clichés and encouraging sentences, he ended on an uninspiring note: 'Well, you're here now, just have to see how you go!'

In a way, he was right. I was confident in my teammates, more so than in myself. I knew that, together, we were good enough. Together, we could win.

Everything about the lead-in to the Grand Final game felt different, excruciatingly drawn out and laborious. It took me twice as long as usual to get across town to the MCG, then there were extensive delays driving onto the site as security checked our ID, searched our cars and then directed us to our designated parking spaces. Time was speeding and crawling at the same time. After what felt like an eternity, I had checked in with the Bulldogs staff, placed my things in my locker and was walking up the race to the MCG.

I had never felt anything like it—the stadium felt alive. It was still two hours before the game, but the crowd was filtering in, tens of thousands of people in the stands towering overhead.

I soaked up the atmosphere. Workers buzzed around, setting up for the pre-game entertainment and the Grand Final sprint, media personalities roamed the ground, and soundchecks echoed through the PA system. *All of this is for us*, I thought. Every single eyeball in the building, every AFL fan across the country, and around the globe, would be watching one thing: the Bulldogs playing the Swans. For the first time, I grasped the magnitude of the event.

With shivers running down my spine, I went back down to the rooms and began my preparation.

Getting my shoulder strapped and my ankle taped went smoothly—barring a slight hold-up while I waited for Jake Stringer to get his extensive blister prevention work done—and then I sat down to listen to Bevo's pre-game speech. He was calm, tapping into the emotions of the group as he had done successfully for the last two years, neither overbearing nor gentle.

'Bring your instruments today, boys,' he told us. He meant that we should show off our talents. Whatever gifts we had as individuals, we needed to bring them out today, for ourselves and for the team.

Everything about the mood, the people in the room, the preparation felt right. I knew we didn't have the best individual players. We had some brilliance in our ranks, but the power of our team was that we were a unit. We moved and flowed together like a flock of starlings—a reference Bevo had often used to describe how we should defend as a team. 'When your teammate moves, you move. Trust each other and play as a single organism.'

Entering the ground for the first warm-up was like walking onto a movie set. Everything was bright and spectacular. Nerves and excitement were evident on my teammates' faces, a mirror of my own feelings. Bonti gave us our mantra, as he often did before games: 'Build intensity slowly, maintain the rage.' Containing our excitement and releasing it at the right time was so important, and we were still a long way away from the first bounce.

Fletcher Roberts and I kicked together in the warm-up, as we always did. We hit one target out of 25 kicks—at least that's how it felt—and exchanged a wry look as if to say, *Well, that couldn't have gone any worse.* Get the bad ones out early, as they say.

Next we returned to the rooms, where we broke into our forward, midfield and backline groups to go over our plans, focus on our goals and calm each other's nerves. We were committing to our task together.

Gia was the perfect mix of excitement and calmness. He gathered all the forwards in a small circle and congratulated us on the year we'd had. 'Just one more, though,' he said.

Our preparation was done. We exited the rooms for the last time before the game started. It was time.

•

The roar as we were announced on the ground was enormous, but I felt strangely calm. I didn't really know what I was feeling, I just knew that we were supposed to be there. I was supposed to be there. It was a comforting thought.

We lined up for the national anthem, and as the final line of 'Advance Australia Fair' was belted out, the crowd broke into an ominous, growing roar—almost 100,000 voices raised in joy and anticipation, deafening. The energy was like lightning, and we players were the lightning rod. I had spent my whole life dreaming of this day and I was finally here.

The first five minutes of the game were insane. The pace was frantic and both teams were applying maximum pressure and attack on the ball. I saw my first opportunity to take a mark coming as Bont wheeled out of a pack and drilled an absolute rocket at me—I could barely track the ball in the air it was moving so fast. But I dropped the easy chest mark. 'Fuck!' I said. Not a good start. But I moved on quickly, looking to my next opportunity. After a frenetic quarter, we gathered at quarter time with the score reading 2.0 (12) to the Swans' 1.2 (8).

In the second quarter, I felt my confidence building. I was finding space on my opponent, I didn't feel the game was too fast, I was always involved and I felt dangerous. A diving mark early in the quarter gave me my first shot on goal. It was as tight an angle as possible: I couldn't really see between the enormous posts at the MCG, and I was on my wrong side.

Despite all that, I was calm. The ball felt comfortable in my hands, grippy enough that I felt completely in control of what was about to happen. There was no wind, and no rush. I walked through my routine, and from the moment the ball hit my left boot I knew it was going to go through. I exploded with excitement—it was exactly what I needed.

Another goal late in the second quarter gave me further boost of energy. Things couldn't be going any better. The game was neck and neck, though, as the quarter was winding down.

I had split my time between the ruck and the forward line, and Roughy and I were working well together. But as I had experienced so many times before in my career, things going perfectly usually meant that they were about to take a turn for the worse.

A ruck contest deep in the Swans' forward 50 led to me being tangled up. I pushed and pulled, before I heard the dreaded *CLUNK* of my shoulder dislocating. In agony, I could only watch as Tom Mitchell roved the ball and kicked an easy snap. I looked to the bench, my shoulder hanging half out of its socket, and tried to signal a change, but no one could hear anything over the roar of the crowd, and I had to take the next centre bounce.

I gathered with the three midfielders. 'Where do you want to hit the ball?' they asked.

'I'll try and get it to nine o'clock,' I said. I couldn't lift my right arm, so I attempted to hit left-handed and made a mess of it, losing the hit-out.

Thankfully, after a couple of minutes of agony, half time sounded and we returned to the rooms. I struggled to listen to Bevo as he addressed the team, watching on while Chris Bell retaped my shoulder, tighter than ever. *I've dealt with this all year—I can do it again*, I thought. The intensity of the game, the opportunity that was in front of us and the noise of the crowd helped to distract me from the pain. Nothing was going to get in the way of us winning—nothing.

•

I was riding the momentum of the first half. I felt like I could mark anything and everything, and that I was never out of the game. I had never felt quite as in control as I did in that moment. I took contested marks and marks on the lead, everything was sticking. We took an eight-point lead into three-quarter time.

At the huddle, Bevo looked at us, every one of us, and said, 'It's right here for you. One more quarter. Don't stop now.' It was almost impossible to hear anything over the noise of the crowd, but his voice rang clear. We were almost there.

The fourth quarter of that Grand Final was the most ruthless, physical period of football I had ever been part of. Buddy Franklin scored for the Swans, then Jake Stringer for us, then George Hewett, then Liam Picken. We couldn't seem to break the Swans, but they couldn't get to the front. Every piece of play I was part of felt like it was worth more than any I'd ever been in before, and my confidence in the team was soaring. The scoreboard said we were only seven points up, but it felt like we had the ascendancy. It felt like our game to me.

Jason Johannisen scored the goal we needed, putting us ahead by two goals—but after an eternity, as we waited looking at the scoreboard, the goal was overturned on review. Still I felt unwavering faith that we would win. I didn't—couldn't—consider the alternative.

With the game once again in the balance, I was playing on autopilot, tracking the ball as it bounced chaotically on the wing. I ran up the middle to help our defenders when a ball came searing in, just in front of me. It was intended for Buddy, and he gathered it but was mown down by Dale Morris. The ball bounced perfectly for me.

At the front edge of the centre square, I swung onto my right foot and looked forward—I couldn't see anything but open grass. The forward 50 was free so I booted the ball as hard as I could. I knew that, at this range, the ball would go right to left, then start fading a bit as it stayed in the air. I had to hit it just right, just inside the left-hand goalpost. My brain calculated all of this in a split second, and as the ball left my laces I knew I had struck it well.

I thought of those endless hours I'd spent with Dad as a kid, in the fading daylight at Mullum Mullum Reserve, practising my kicking. I thought of those hot summers, training with him in Anglesea. I must have practised this shot on goal a thousand times. I watched the ball sail exactly as I had hoped, and I started to pace sideways, hoping, praying that it would go through.

The ball landed just shy of the goal line, but I knew that with the power I had put into it, it was still moving. It bobbled up, as though for dramatic effect, and then crossed the goal line.

The noise was unfathomable. It was so loud that I couldn't really hear it, but I felt it shaking the ground beneath my feet.

I didn't know what had happened, but I knew it was truly incredible. I ran, arms outstretched, my heart exploding.

A few moments passed before I even realised that Toby McLean had jumped on my back and I was carrying him. My teammates mobbed me in my moment of triumph, their excitement overflowing—all but one player.

Liam Picken grabbed me from the pack of players, holding my jumper and shaking me back down to earth. 'Keep your head in the game!' he screamed. 'It's not over!'

He was right. We didn't know how much time was left, which meant there was still time for the Swans to make a run. But a missed set shot from the Swans and a late goal from Picken sealed the match. The siren sounded and pandemonium erupted.

●

The blur of people I interacted with after the game was incredible. Fans, players, staff, friends and family, moments of bliss in among the chaos, feelings so huge I could not put them into words.

At one point I sat down with Joel Hamling in the middle of the MCG, trying to grasp the magnitude of the moment, wondering how it could ever get better than this. At another moment I threw my arms around Mitch Wallis and Lin Jong, heartbroken that they couldn't be a part of it. I bear-hugged my little sister in the change rooms, in the middle of a radio interview, surrounded by strangers. I heard my mother say she loved me with tears in her eyes. I saw the pride in my dad's eyes and the smile across his face, more pride than I'd ever seen from him in my entire life.

As the lights dimmed and the crowds disappeared, we returned as a team to the empty MCG, with the Premiership Cup in the middle of the centre circle and a beer in everyone's hand. We sang our club song, 'Sons of the West'. It was an emotional time, everyone hugging, smiling and laughing. There was chaos behind us and more chaos ahead, but this was a rare moment of joyous peace between us, as we reflected on what we had accomplished together.

I looked out across the dark MCG, barely able to comprehend what had just happened, what I had achieved, what we had achieved and how far we had come. It felt like everything in my life would get better from this point on—that my troubles, worries and fears were behind me. *I'm an AFL Premiership player now—what can anyone say?* It felt like my career had begun again, that I would leave the criticism and the bullshit behind, that I could just be me again.

I looked around at my teammates, these champions, and felt like I was a part of something truly special. We had come together to create history. I never wanted the moment to end.

10

STRESS TEST

The frenzy that followed the Grand Final was like nothing I had ever experienced. Even just leaving the ground was an arduous process; trying to get everyone on the bus to head to our after-match function at the Melbourne Convention Centre was a debacle.

Players were stuck behind, hugging family, grabbing clothes, organising belongings and trying to work out where to store their keys so they could come back and pick up their cars later in the next week (or a few weeks later, depending on how long the celebrations lasted).

I managed to sneak one of my great friends, Owinda Weerawardena, into the function along with my parents, and together we sat through what felt like very long-winded formalities before the team was presented on stage.

I normally hated those kinds of events, their stiffness and the endless speeches and all the glad-handing I was expected to do. But this felt different. I was so proud of our team, and was thoroughly enjoying not being the disappointment for once. I revelled in the glory of being an AFL Premiership winner, and welcomed the external validation that was heaped upon us.

The formal proceedings finished with a speech from our club president, Peter Gordon. He had been dedicated to the Bulldogs for decades and had taken a great leap of faith in bringing me to the club, and it was wonderful to see him feel such joy in that historic moment. I had seen him on the ground right after we won, and I will never forget the smile that was on his face.

As Peter spoke, I was standing at the bar with Dad, apart from the crowd. We exchanged quiet comments, whispering and smiling—the first moments alone we had shared since the end of the game. It felt amazing, as though every moment we'd ever shared had brought us to this one, where Dad was gushing with pride and joy.

Peter continued speaking, noting the many, many contributors to the club's success, and small points of personal pride he'd experienced in his journey as president. He made a happy reference to my performance; Dad and I chuckled and raised our glasses from the back of the function room.

When the club dinner was done, I said goodbye to my family and left for the after-party—a very big night out with the team in the middle of the CBD. I found myself wandering back through the front door of my home in the early hours of the morning, with only a couple of hours to try to sleep before I was due at the club for a family day event. I was hungover, gluey-eyed and sleep-deprived when I left the house again, but with the help of a pair of sunglasses, I pulled myself together.

The ocean of red, white and blue at Whitten Oval was epic, and my hangover was instantly cured. A sea of the Bulldogs faithful, 40,000 strong, had come to celebrate the win with us. We were presented one by one on stage, and when my time to step up arrived, I looked out at the crowd in awe. *This can't be real, can it? Twenty-four hours ago I was preparing for a game of football, and now look . . .*

Bulldogs fans, young and old, screamed and cheered as we watched on from an upper balcony attached to the administration section of the club. After a brief but glorious ceremony, I left Whitten Oval and continued on to the Railway Hotel in Yarraville, which was still painted in our club colours. A day of indulgence with family and friends followed, another late night, and then another early morning for me. I had to be up at 7 a.m. to see a surgeon in Hawthorn, with my shoulder surgery scheduled for the following week. My teammate Caleb Daniel had to have his shoulder done as well, so he stayed at my house that night.

My phone was flat when I woke up—I hadn't had the presence of mind to charge it when I got home—and Caleb had only a tiny amount of battery left. We tried to book a taxi on his phone but it died before the taxi arrived, so we found ourselves wandering the streets of Port Melbourne, trying to find the taxi we'd ordered, knowing it was around somewhere. Eventually, Caleb asked a poor stranger if he could use her phone so he could call the driver. Luckily for us, she obliged.

Caleb and I had both been told definitively that our surgeries were going ahead. Initially, the club had scheduled our operations for the Monday or Tuesday following the Grand Final, but in the aftermath of victory, Caleb and I banded together and told the wonderful club doctors, Gary Zimmerman and Jake Landsberger, that we would most definitely *not* be getting surgery that week. 'I'm serious, don't book us in, Zim, we won't be there,' Caleb said. They laughed and agreed to give us another week.

Unfortunately, our early-morning appointment meant we were late to the beginning of Mad Monday, which was a big no-no, though we survived the wrath of organiser (and team dad) Dale Morris. The day was filled with laughter, ridiculous games and fun, while our Grand Final victory played on repeat around the pub. Then, before I knew it, it was Tuesday, and we were due at the club for our exit interviews with the coaches. Mine was with Gia and Bevo, as well as the incoming forwards coach, Ash Hansen.

'Tommy! How you feeling?' Bevo asked, with a smile on

his face. The coaches all looked tired—it had been a huge few days for them too.

'Not too bad,' I answered. 'Bit tired, but pretty good, all things considered. My shoulder is a bit rough.'

We chatted away, with both small talk and discussion of more serious topics, but the conversation ended on a note of real optimism.

'It's such a powerful thing to see you overcome some challenges this year, and to end it with an incredible performance in the most important game of your career,' Ash said. 'I'm super-excited to work with you next season.'

I felt the same way, though I was finding it hard to process much by that stage. *Next year is my year*, I thought briefly, before returning home to rest.

I celebrated my 21st birthday that night in Port Melbourne, at a different Railway Hotel, surrounded by close mates from the Bulldogs, as well as friends and family. It was the first decent meal I had eaten in days—definitely the first that hadn't come out of a fryer. I couldn't have asked for a better night, or a better week, to hit that milestone.

By the Wednesday morning, I was well and truly exhausted, but there would be no reprieve anytime soon. Our duties at the club began early, with a signing session scheduled for the morning that would last four or five hours. We signed jumpers, posters, footballs, photos—signature after signature, over a thousand individual items. To add to my woes, we were due to present ourselves to a record-breaking crowd at the Crown Palladium that night for our club best-and-fairest awards.

For the first time since the Grand Final, I just wanted to stop. I wanted to take some time to rest and recover, to see my family and spend some time with my friends. I was expecting a brutal barrage of photos and signatures at the Crown event, and I felt dread at the prospect of incessant chats and handshaking.

Anna came to the event with me, a beautiful and supportive partner. But it was quickly evident to her that she was merely in the way. I became exceedingly frustrated with the way fans would push her aside, or ask her to take photos for them, and I didn't want to subject her to that sort of treatment.

As soon as the main ceremony was over, we tried to leave—but before we could escape, more people approached me, more conversations started, more requests for photographs were made. Anna was forced to walk ahead of me, separated by the fans. Most of them were nice and supportive, but a fair share had had too much to drink and were obnoxious and rude, and my patience was running thin.

Just then, a coterie club member who I had known for some time approached me. 'Ah, Boyd, get a photo with me, would ya?' he slurred. He was hanging onto my arm, holding me in place. 'I never rated ya. I always thought you were no good, but thankfully you played well when ya needed to. That's what we pay ya for!'

His condescension was unbearable, and I snapped. 'Well, it must look easy from the fucking stands, I guess!'

I walked away from him to find Anna, politely declining any more requests for signatures or photographs, angry that the day had ended so sourly.

The incident stayed with me over the next few days. *What have I done? Will I get in trouble?* I wondered. It was uncharacteristic of me to respond in the way I had, but the guy was being such an idiot. If I'd been rude to him, it was only because he'd given me good reason. Still, I fretted over it. I couldn't comprehend how someone could think it was okay to give me such a backhanded compliment, given what our team had just achieved.

For the most part, the week had been a wonderful celebration at a club so long deprived of success. The gracious, kind and caring fans far outnumbered the rude ones, but it was the behaviour of the rude ones that stuck with me. A bad taste lingered in my mouth at the memory of how Anna had been shoved aside so that strangers could have a photo with me. I'd barely had a chance to talk to her that night.

In my memory, the bright smiles and laughter from that night started to become blurry, stained by my irritation and discomfort.

•

My surgery took place the following Monday. A significant reconstruction of my right shoulder had been on the cards for such a long time. During the past season, Chris Bell came around after every game and asked each player if they had any concerns. 'Any issues, Tom?' he would ask.

'My back was a bit crook, and my shoulder came out a couple of times,' I'd usually respond.

'Yep, we'll get that fixed up at the end of the year,' he'd say. He stopped bothering to write it down. It wasn't that he didn't care—there just weren't any real options, except to tape it up, do strength work and wait.

I hadn't anticipated how painful the surgery would be. In my hospital room afterwards, I was in more pain than I could have imagined, a horrendous throbbing and aching that the medication failed to alleviate. No amount of distraction or support from Anna could help me.

To make matters worse, Caleb was apparently feeling fine. He wandered down to my hospital room with a smile on his face, having had a slightly different shoulder reconstruction, and said he only had a bit of a dull ache.

My pain subsided after a few days and sleepless nights. Because of the surgery, I had my arm in an elevated sling, propped at a 45-degree angle in front of my body. Mentally, I began to prepare for my next surgery, a much less invasive cleanout of my ankle, which had been troublesome since my final year of junior football. That procedure came a week later.

After it was done, I left the hospital in a wheelchair, unable to use my right arm or walk on my left foot. Within three weeks of being at my athletic peak, I was now a mess of bandages and slings. My muscles were already showing signs of atrophy, and flab was starting to grow around my belly.

There were only seven weeks or so between the Grand Final and the start of the preseason, and they were slipping by fast. I realised then that my routine would be no different now that I was a Premiership player, and I began to worry, as usual, about how I would get back to full fitness. One day, back at the club, a throwaway comment about us both looking 'a bit full in the face' left both Caleb and me feeling anxious about how we'd stay in shape while being on the sidelines for the foreseeable future.

All I had planned for the off-season was a quick trip to Bali. Mum and Dad flew over with me and Anna, and Owinda joined us later. I was in desperate need of a break, emotionally and physically drained from the season just gone, and I could sense the new season quickly approaching. I planned to train in the heat, doing what I could to keep fit, but I was unable to run, swim or surf, or do any other form of upper-body cross-training. I resigned myself to using the elliptical trainer in the resort gym, with one arm by my side, and I treaded as far as I could each morning—as much as my ankle could tolerate.

Mentally, I wasn't in a good place. My injuries were weighing on my mind, and the frustration I felt that

I couldn't maintain my fitness was aggravating. Sleep was hard enough to manage with my arm in a sling even without that building tension, and my mood quickly deteriorated. I argued with Anna, and with my parents. All in all, I was no fun to be around.

My mood didn't improve when I returned to Melbourne. The off-season was almost over, but I felt like the last season had only just ended. As the date to go back to the club drew closer, I started to feel extraordinarily anxious. I had a creeping sense that I'd run out of time. I didn't have time to get fit enough. I didn't have time to get my shoulder right. I didn't have time to get myself ready for the challenge of a new season.

I saw growing speculation in the media that my Grand Final performance was the key that would unlock my potential as a top-tier player—'It will be just like Tom Hawkins in 2011!' Everyone was discussing the similarities in the arcs of our careers, and I was scared of disappointing them.

That feeling of stress and urgency continued to mount as preseason got underway, and I watched unhappily from the sidelines as my teammates began training without me.

•

The spotlight on our Grand Final success only intensified the worries I had about the season ahead, especially when

I considered all the obstacles we'd had to overcome along the way. *How did we even get through all that?* I wondered.

Winning a Premiership had set a new bar for success and joy in my football career, and it was so high that in my mind it seemed impossible to reach. Surely we were never going to have a run of success like that again. The expectation in the footy world was that we would be in contention again in 2017 as we had such a young and promising list, but now we had a target on our back.

When I thought about it, the season ahead didn't feel promising at all. It seemed long and taxing, especially as I would be starting from behind because of my compromised preseason. My energy and motivation levels were already depleted, which only led to more doubt and dread. I felt like I was running on fumes already.

I worried about how I was feeling, and how it would impact my performance going forward, and my sleep quickly began to deteriorate. It happened so fast, in fact, that it was dizzying. I felt like I was cycling downward, like a snowball running down a mountain, picking up more momentum and size as I continued on. My thoughts were a nonstop loop, where my doubts about myself fed my fears about the season, which fed my stress and sleeplessness, which fed my doubts—around and around I went.

Before long, the anxiety I felt towards football was unbearable. It was always at its worst at night, when I tried to sleep, and again when I woke up in the morning. I couldn't work out why I was so stressed—*I've just won a Premiership*—but it was exhausting.

My first panic attack came as I was driving through Port Melbourne, on my way to training. As I approached the shipping containers at the docks, just before joining the Westgate Freeway, my heart started to hammer in my chest like it was going to explode. I was sweating profusely and couldn't calm myself down.

I pulled over on the side of the road, gasping for air. I had never been so scared in my life. *Am I having a heart attack?* I managed to calm myself enough to restart the car and get to training. I didn't say a word to anyone at the club, but I knew I needed help.

Our club psychologist was Lisa Stevens. I had met with her a few times since joining the Bulldogs in late 2014, mostly to talk about elite performance psychology—how to manage my mind, to stay in the moment while playing, to work through a goalkicking routine. In 2016, we had talked through some of the challenges I was facing, and she'd been instrumental in building my confidence in myself and the team as the year progressed. But I had never really shared anything with her below surface-level interactions. I loved the fact that she understood the club but could be objective about things, because she worked at arm's length from it. She was a sounding board with great insight who didn't feel the need to take sides.

After the success of the 2016 season, I was convinced that

I wouldn't need any more help—that I was a 'made man' of sorts after winning a Premiership. After all, wasn't that the whole reason we played football in the first place? So I didn't go back to see Lisa at the start of preseason. But in her weekly club visits, she would always smile when we passed in the gym or the hallway and ask me how I was going.

As I began to feel worse and worse, I started avoiding interactions with her as much as possible. I felt like she would be able to see through the smiles I was putting on for others and would notice I was actually struggling, and I was afraid that admitting my issues to someone would make them real.

But over time, Lisa managed to get some conversations going with me. They were friendly and informal, but eventually I began to book in for fifteen minutes of time with her when she was at the club. I didn't want to do it regularly. I wasn't worried about how my teammates would react—we were all encouraged to see her because her work was so effective—but if I was seeing her regularly, then it felt like an acknowledgement that I was losing control. It meant that I wasn't myself anymore, and that I wasn't strong enough to cope.

For years, I had baked the idea into my mind that the pressure of performing didn't bother me—that it was part and parcel of being an AFL player, and that the scrutiny that came my way was something I had signed up for when I took that contract. These were things I had been telling myself since I was eighteen. If I embraced Lisa's support, I felt I would be making all those ideas into lies. But things only continued to get worse.

In one of our chats at the club, Lisa mentioned that I could see her for a proper session at her office during the week, and I knew I had to do it. I couldn't see another way forward, and I didn't have anyone else that I could talk to. So before the 2017 preseason was over, I began to see her every week, trying to work through the mess of what was happening inside my head. *Why am I so uncomfortable in public? Why am I having panic attacks? Why am I sad all the time?* I couldn't comprehend why I felt this way when I had the life I did.

I had experienced the highest of highs only months earlier. I was a physically healthy, very well paid 21-year-old athlete, doing exactly what I'd dreamed I would do when I was growing up. The disconnection between what I had and how I felt about myself filled me with guilt and shame. I didn't want to feel that way anymore. And I wanted to feel better before the AFL season got underway.

Lisa was wonderful, but my issues continued. Every morning, driving to the club, I worried about having another panic attack, either in the car or during our morning meeting. My guts churned and I was constantly jittery. Most days I did not have a panic attack, but the fear of it happening was almost as bad.

When I got through the morning, training would alleviate some of my stress. I exercised my stress away, though

I felt far from my best on the field. Then the fatigue from training left me with a whole new issue: the stress I felt before training, combined with the physical exertion, left me feeling extraordinarily low, as though my energy levels had been depleted. I limped through most afternoon sessions, away from the watchful gaze of the coaches, needing multiple coffees through the afternoon to help me concentrate.

When preseason came to an end, I had to focus everything I could on the upcoming season. I had run out of time to deal with my issues; now I had to concentrate on football.

For the first time in my AFL career, I was a certainty to start in the side in Round 1. I had got back to full training as soon as I could and was performing relatively well in a new ruck-focused role. I needed to build my match fitness, but the coaching staff were reasonably positive about where I was at.

I didn't share their optimism. The year ahead looked long and arduous to me. We were supposed to be the reigning champions, the toast of the town, but I felt just the opposite. I was in a war, battling my private demons while struggling to do the job that I was getting paid so much to do.

•

Our Round 1 match against Collingwood was a nightmare, even though we won. I was selected as our sole ruckman, which pitted me against Brodie Grundy and Mason Cox, who had me exhausted from the first quarter. Besides the preliminary final the year before, I had never really had to ruck on my own, and when I had it was only because Jordan Roughead was injured. I tried hard and competed in the ruck, but the rest of my game was compromised because of the added workload.

Abuse flowed from the stands, and from opposition players. I'd heard it all before, but now it felt different. Criticism relating to my contract had always made me uncomfortable, but now it was far more frustrating. The abuse from one player in particular took me by surprise— *You haven't won a Premiership! Who are you to have a go at me?*—but I was mostly frustrated with myself. Why was I so naive to think that on-field challenges like this were going to go away? I had spent so much of the preseason focusing on my own internal issues, wrongly thinking that all the external challenges and criticisms were in the past.

After the game, I saw Anna. She seemed a little flat and irritated but was reluctant to tell me why. Eventually, she explained that she had been sitting in front of a Bulldogs supporter who had spent the game abusing me. It had taken some time before one of her friends turned around and said something, only for the fan to respond that they were 'only joking'.

I felt responsible. It was my fault that she'd had to go through that, and I hated that she was upset by it. I told her not to worry about it, they were just some idiot—but it only added to the weight on my shoulders that night. I had never felt so bad after a win in my entire career.

●

We unveiled our Premiership flag against Sydney ahead of our first home game of the year. Not a single spark of positive emotion came over me when it unfurled. The coaches had made it very clear that last year was behind us, and winning this year was now all that mattered.

We had another win, but it didn't feel like it had before. It wasn't just me—it couldn't be, as our whole team felt different. We had always celebrated and enjoyed each victory; every win at AFL level is like climbing a mountain, so it's important to savour each one. But we were struggling to find the same satisfaction, because now winning was an expectation, and so it never felt like enough. Without the feeling of joy that I once had when we won, playing felt pointless, like I was putting myself through the agony of an AFL game for nothing. I tried to remind myself that the money alone was worth it, that didn't work. The two things didn't feel connected at all. *Why am I still doing this?*

As the season progressed, the load of being our only ruckman began to weigh on me, physically as much as mentally. It took all my fortitude to prepare myself to ruck for a full game every week, knowing how important it was for my teammates. After our success in 2016 utilising a 'third man up' in the ruck, the AFL changed the rules to make that illegal, so it was even more important that our ruckman competed well every time. I felt a great obligation to Bont, Libba, Dahl, Wal—to all of my teammates, really—to do a good job for them, and I sensed their frustration when I came up short.

Outside of the team, criticism was mounting against the strategy of making me the only ruckman, and the fact that I was being convincingly beaten most weeks became a talking point. Bevo defended me aggressively, but the truth is I felt out of my depth a lot of the time. I had good games and bad, but figuring out how best to help the team was challenging. Some weeks I would get lots of hit-outs but not much of the ball; other weeks it would be the opposite. I tried to strike a balance between playing to my strengths as a smaller, more agile ruckman and competing well against the traditional rucks, but that balance was hard to find.

•

After the 2016 Grand Final, my notoriety had grown considerably. I was now getting spotted by people in the street far more than before. People had always noticed my height, but they were connecting the dots now and had no qualms about calling out to me in public.

'Boydie!'

'Boyd's kicked a goal! Fuck!'

'The million-dollar man!'

'You're shit!'

It wasn't all bad, but the bad seemed to outweigh the good—or maybe I was just perceiving it that way. At times it was hard to tell what was real. The amount of discomfort this public attention brought me is hard to describe, especially when it happened and I was with friends outside of football. 'It must be great that everyone notices you,' they would say, or 'Is it awesome being a Premiership player?'

I always answered that the same way: 'Nothing really changes. I'll probably reflect back on it when I'm retired and appreciate it more.'

The truth was that things had changed, but not in the way people thought.

My life was different now. For one thing, I had genuinely impacted the lives of many supporters. Time and time again I would run into older Bulldogs fans who had made the trek out to Whitten Oval to watch us train or to catch up with friends at the nearby Barkers Café, and I knew that the Western Bulldogs—or the Footscray Football Club, as it had been for most of their lives—meant unimaginably more to them than it could ever mean to me.

The penny dropped when I met a lady who must have been at least 80, and who said something so powerful that it left me speechless. She approached me at Barkers Café one morning while I was getting a coffee, and grabbed me with both hands and looked straight into my eyes. 'Thank you for the Premiership,' she said. 'I never thought I would see one, now I can die happy.'

I just couldn't fathom how football could mean so much to anyone, but she wasn't alone. In late 2016 ex-players, coaches and staff had come out in droves to express their joy at our historic victory, and messages flooded into the club from the families of lifetime members—including some who had passed away shortly after the Grand Final but 'with a smile on their face'.

So on the one hand I was being criticised, online, in the media and by random strangers on the street. Simultaneously, I was being told that I had changed people's lives in an unimaginably good way. Adding to the whiplash, no matter what I had done in 2016, my job now was to play well in the next game—that's what I was paid for. I was simply overwhelmed by the noise surrounding what I did for a living. Tom Boyd, AFL Footballer—that's all people could see when they looked at me, with no concern for who I was, what I cared about or enjoyed, or the people I cared for. I so badly wanted people to know that I was a good person, worth talking to, not someone who deserved to be yelled at.

My job soaked up so much of my energy that I started avoiding situations where I would have to be seen and talked to. I stopped leaving the house for things other than necessities. I avoided social events, and if I did go, I often left early, overwhelmed and anxious. I became great at making up excuses, at skipping things and avoiding situations that might cause me distress. Just like in my earlier years, when I'd watched Norwood matches from the other side of the oval, I isolated myself, hoping that if I could avoid my issues for long enough, they might disappear.

•

The 2017 season wasn't slowing down. After starting with four wins and one loss, we then lost three of our next four games, and the pressure was mounting on both our team and our coach. The media talked about a 'Premiership hangover', and though it wasn't part of our conversations within the club, a distinct flatness seemed to be affecting the group. Every victory felt like a relief, and every loss a disaster.

I quickly got stuck in a negative thought pattern: *We can't do anything right*. It was as though the air in the building was stale, like we were recycling fuel from last year that didn't have the same horsepower as previously. We had the desire but couldn't find the connectivity or flow that we needed to carry us through the tough moments of a long AFL season. Everything was a grind.

Adding to my worries, my sleep issues had got far worse. I wasn't sleeping well at all. The nights before games were sometimes completely sleepless. I asked Anna to start spending more time at her own apartment, in the hope that sleeping alone might help. It didn't—and it only upset

Anna, as she felt me pushing her away. That just made me feel more guilty.

My lack of sleep before games was making everything harder, and wearing my body down. My aches and pains weren't recovering like they used to, and I began to have issues with my back that were so severe I sometimes had to pull out of training sessions during the week. Every week I felt less capable of carrying the ruck load by myself. I didn't want to get to the point where I broke down early in a game, or got dominated by a bigger, more prepared opponent, as that could cost our team a win.

The first people to notice my gradual decline were our physios, Chris Bell and Sara Hasani in particular. They saw my back issues becoming more significant week after week. 'Are you going alright? Sleeping okay?' they asked.

I decided to be honest with them about my sleep. It was bad, I said. I rarely slept well anymore and was seeing Lisa regularly.

Chris and Sara were genuinely concerned, and I knew they wanted to help me, but they were hamstrung by deadlines. It was their job to get me to a place where I could play each week; they couldn't do much other than support me through my training schedule and give me encouragement.

As the season wore on, I felt my fitness levels dropping. I was only training once a week, then playing games on the weekend. For much of each week I was restricted to Pilates and swimming, and a special weights program for my back.

I was protecting it during the week so that I could play on weekends, but each week I lost a little bit of strength, a little bit of fitness. And the impact of our games on my body became just that bit more severe.

Somehow I was managing to perform my role—in fact, I was even showing signs of improvement in my ability to help the midfielders. I played what was arguably my best game for the year down at Kardinia Park in Round 9. We lost, but I had twenty disposals, two goals and 33 hit-outs in the game. But it didn't matter—I felt the same flat, empty feeling I'd had for weeks.

Once upon a time, I would have been proud to have put in a good performance in a team loss, knowing that I had 'done my job'. I would hide this satisfaction from my teammates, but I would feel it. That just wasn't the case anymore.

The following week, against St Kilda, things did not go as well. Early in the game, a shooting pain in my calf stopped me from running. I had never really had a significant soft-tissue injury, but I was certain that this was what they felt like. I came to the bench, was assessed and managed to hobble through the remainder of the game. We won easily, thankfully, but I was sore afterwards. I really needed the bye we had the following week.

The diagnosis of my calf strain surprised me—there was no tear, just a little bit of bleeding, so it was nothing to be too concerned about. Defensively, I told the physio that there was no way in hell I had imagined the pain—I hadn't made it up.

Calmly, Chris said, 'It's probably coming from your back, mate. It's been playing up for weeks and you've had tightness all through that side of your body.'

'But you can feel it right?' I pressed him. I had to know that he understood how sore it was.

'Yes, mate, there's a huge band of tightness right here.' He pressed down and pain shot through my leg.

I was relieved. I almost wished that my calf had been torn clearly. I didn't want anyone thinking that I was a cop-out.

A plan was put in place to get me back playing after our bye, but I ended up missing the following week as well. I wanted my calf to be right. I knew I couldn't expect it to be 100 per cent, but it couldn't be 75 per cent because I would be spending most of the game in the ruck.

The week I sat out, the Bulldogs played in Sydney against the Swans, a team we'd beaten consistently for the past few years. Bob Murphy invited a few of our injured players over to his house to watch the game, which was a train wreck from the beginning: we lost by 46 points but it should have been more. Tom Campbell, Marcus Adams, Bob and I chatted about how challenging the week ahead would be. A loss like that would mean a response from the coaches and some aggressive training sessions—it would be 'a line in the sand moment', as they say.

A panic attack started as I drove home, and it got worse

and worse as I travelled along Punt Road towards my house. I had the heater on but I was shivering and sweating at the same time, and my heart rate skyrocketed. I was aching suddenly, like I had the flu.

I took a shower when I arrived home, hoping that would calm me down, but it didn't work. I writhed in bed, anxiety ridden and terrified, pouring with sweat. When morning came, I struggled to work out what was real and what wasn't. I was exhausted—and I had a training session to attend.

•

I returned to the AFL side to play the following week, which brought a blowout loss to Melbourne. I hadn't played well, but it certainly wasn't my worst performance. The worst thing about the result that day was how I felt about it. I didn't feel despair; I felt nothing. It seemed unimportant and small compared to what I was dealing with off the field.

It wasn't that I didn't care, but that I couldn't. I'd had back and hamstring spasms during the game but had played through them, with limited movement, every jump sending shocks through my body as I landed.

Chris Bell spoke to me after the game, his face furrowed. 'We need to do something to get this right, mate. We can't keep having your back be such an issue out there.' Yet again, we set up a plan to get me to a place where I could play again.

Soon after the match, one of my teammates, Travis Cloke, who'd joined us that year after a long career at Collingwood, announced that he was taking an 'indefinite break from playing to manage mental health issues'. I was shocked. I had no idea that a guy like him, who looked absolutely bulletproof and had been one of the best full-forwards in the league, could be dealing with something so troubling below the surface.

I struggled to compute what it meant. I hadn't spoken much with him, other than in passing and at training, and I was consumed with my own issues. But the next time I saw Lisa, she asked me how I felt about it.

I was conflicted. I knew nothing of Travis's circumstances, I said, so I had no real insight. I could only imagine it was serious if he was taking leave.

'Are you worried because now you can't consider the possibility of taking time off?' she asked me.

I thought about this. Lisa and I had been discussing a break for weeks, but hadn't got to the stage of making a solid plan. Being injured had bought me some time, but now taking time off felt more difficult. *What would people think of the Bulldogs? What would people think of me?* My concerns extended beyond myself. I knew that what I was going through wasn't the club's fault—it had taken a very long time for me to arrive at this point—but with two players taking time off, it would look like a trend. It felt like my options had shrunk again.

The next couple of weeks were brutal. A sleepless night once or twice a week became most nights. Before long, I couldn't remember the last time I had slept properly. I was seeing Lisa and talking to her as much as possible, but it didn't seem to help. I felt sick constantly, and my back and body ached from tossing and turning through the night.

It became harder to hide my issues at the club, as well. My short-term memory had become so bad that I would forget everything, from what exercise I was supposed to be doing in the gym to what time I was meant to have treatments.

Things turned from bad to worse when I came home to find Anna in tears, my antidepressant medications on the table in front of her. A doctor had prescribed them for me, after Lisa's suggestion, but I hadn't told my girlfriend. I hadn't intended to hide them from her—I'd left them on the bench—but at the same time, I wasn't planning to address the issue with her either.

'Why didn't you tell me?' Anna asked. 'I didn't know it was this bad.'

'Don't worry,' I told her. 'It's going to be okay.'

I wanted to reassure her, but I honestly didn't believe that anymore.

•

The past few months had been a merry-go-round of different doctors and appointments as I tried to get better. But nothing seemed to work. I slept less, connected less, smiled less and shrunk down until I was a shadow of who I'd once been.

I knew, first of all, that I needed to sleep—that nothing was going to improve without getting that under control. I felt like I was driving at night, exhausted but wide awake, all the time. It seemed like the doctors were talking at me, and in every session their focus changed, but my symptoms didn't. I had no sleep, no joy and an abundance of anxiety.

Somehow, through all of this, I managed to get myself into a position where the club had no choice but to send me back to play in the VFL, with a plan to get me back to the AFL side quickly. Once upon a time, the idea that I was needed in the AFL side would have felt good—it wasn't something that I'd always had—yet now I found it overwhelming, even frightening. My body did not feel capable of getting through a game of AFL football, not with the array of issues I was trying to navigate. My mental struggles had fed my illness and injury, and vice versa.

As the days ticked down to my return to the AFL, my anxiety ramped up. I didn't sleep at all and I spent my days in an unbearable state of discomfort, feeling like I had exhausted all my options. I sat alone in my small house in Albert Park, with the rain pelting against my windows, not knowing what would happen next. A million thoughts ran through my head.

How did I get here?

What is wrong with me?

Why is this happening?
What is the point?
I've gotta call someone.

I called Lisa. For the first time, I was completely honest with her about how bad things had become. I told her in detail how trapped I felt. How terrified.

Calm as always, she talked through it with me. She sat in the moment with me, as difficult as that was. I was at my lowest point.

'What do you want to do? Do you need a break?' Lisa asked.

'I don't know.'

'When are you supposed to play next?'

'This weekend.'

'Do you think you can get through the game?'

'I really don't know.'

We continued talking, trying to work out what my options were. She sensed how hesitant I was to step back from my duties at the club. I didn't want to let my team-mates down. I had never taken a game off in my life—it felt wrong—but I simply couldn't keep going the way I was.

•

I went to Lisa's office. We spent hours together that day, talking through all the things that were going on, sorting through the mess that was my mental state. She didn't want me to be on my own that evening, but I assured her that Anna would be there for me.

We met again the next morning and finally decided that what I needed was a week off. The top priority was my well-being, not a game of football. But it was easy to agree to that with Lisa. What came next was much harder.

The following day, I met with all the key stakeholders in the football department; Lisa and the medical staff were there too. I was extremely worried about how they would react to their big-name recruit being brought to his knees by an invisible problem, but Lisa took the reins. She had already briefed many of the people involved.

To my surprise, the club responded with full-throated support.

'We had no idea it was this bad.'

'We will obviously do everything we can to support you.'

'Anything you need.'

I was thankful—this made the process easier. The next hurdle was dealing with the media.

'Now, Tom, what would you like us to say? Because we will need to make a statement at some point,' they told me. 'We can fend them off for a couple of days, but they will begin to ask questions, especially when you don't play this weekend.'

We discussed the options: we could come up with a cover story, take a strong defensive line, or simply not comment at all.

'I don't want to lie,' I said. There didn't seem to be any point in trying to hide what was going on—people were going to find out one way or another. *These things never stay under wraps*, I thought.

But it wasn't just that. I felt less physically capable of completing a game of AFL football than I ever had before. I couldn't concentrate, I wasn't confident in my body, and after months and months of stress and sleep issues, I was unable to play.

'Tell them the truth,' I said. 'There's no point in disguising it.'

As the meeting wrapped up, the club told me to take some time to consider it and let them know what I wanted to do.

'That went okay, I thought,' Lisa said when we met again later.

I agreed. It was never going to be pleasant; it had gone as well as it possibly could have. Thankfully, it hadn't taken too long, as I was struggling to keep up with the conversation after another sleepless night.

'Have you thought any more about a statement?' she asked. 'Just because I know they will come asking me, sooner rather than later.'

I told her I had. I still felt the same way about being honest. In fact, I hadn't been so sure about anything in a while. All people needed to know was that I was unable to play, that the reason I was unable to play was because I was injured, and that the source of the injury was my mental health issues.

In my mind, this made perfect sense. I had avoided the issue for as long as I could remember, hiding how I felt, telling people I was fine and I wasn't struggling with the pressure or the criticism. I had pretended that I could handle anything that came my way. I'd pretended that I still loved football, and that things were going to get better. It had only served to make things worse. I was finally ready to just deal with it.

•

The statement was crafted by the club and circulated confidentially to people I trusted, including my parents. Mum was beside herself, but she had known something was going on. Dad tried to understand. 'It reads fine to me,' he said.

Anna was relieved, and unbelievably supportive. I was glad that she was feeling better about it, as I was sure my problems had been weighing heavily on her.

The statement read:

Western Bulldogs forward Tom Boyd has been provided a leave of absence from the Club while he receives treatment for clinical depression.

Tom has managed his illness in conjunction with the Bulldogs' medical staff for an extended period, and will continue to receive the Club's full support as he works through this challenge.

Tom has indicated a desire to return to playing as soon as possible, and the Club will work closely with Tom and the Bulldogs' medical staff to determine a suitable time for reintegration into the training program.

The Club will continue to provide an extensive support framework to help Tom manage his illness and asks for the respect for Tom's position during this time.

A new plan was set in motion, with a timeline for me to return to play. The definitive nature of it scared me. I had no reason to think that I would be 'fixed' in six weeks, or two months, or two years. It had taken me a long time to sink to the bottom, and I had no idea how long it would take me to get back up.

For the first two weeks, I didn't attend the club at all. Messages of support poured in from the players, coaches and staff—everyone wanted me to know they were thinking of me. I felt like I had relieved them of a burden, in a way. It must have been difficult to deal with me at my worst, not to mention with all the scrutiny my poor performances had brought on the football club. Although I had stepped away from Whitten Oval, I still had support from the club—the player development manager and the high performance manager met me twice a week at Albert Park for light training sessions, to keep my muscles moving.

When I could, I escaped to Anglesea and stayed with Anna and her family. Her mum, Ingrid, was particularly welcoming. I wanted to be away from everything. I knew I couldn't hide forever, but Anglesea had been a refuge for me since I was young, and it gave Anna and me the chance to turn down the volume on all the noise that came in the wake of my announcement.

However, it wasn't long before I was expected back at the club to train, in whatever way I could manage. I had a full schedule of appointments with my psychologist, psychiatrist and doctor over the next few weeks, and did some light running and weights, at minimal exertion levels, on the fringes of the club's training sessions. I felt like I was physically injured.

In reality, I was. My issues had manifested in the heaviness and exhaustion of my limbs, in my endless back pain and my jittery, sleep-deprived body. That was why I missed games. But the physical injuries were only symptoms of the real problem.

•

Over the next two months, I slowly reintegrated back into the club. I had huge support from the team. People were genuinely understanding, which took me by surprise, but it was still incredibly difficult. My recovery was slow. I still wasn't sleeping, and I was still suffering from extreme levels of anxiety and low mood. Soon enough, the question of when I would return to play became louder.

I was struggling to balance my physical training with my health appointments, while also trialling a different anti-depressant medication; it was overwhelming how many different commitments and contacts I had to remember. Soon, I began to feel impatience from the club, and some pressure to return to a full training schedule. In turn, I began to feel guilty for not doing my job. At the same time, I knew my mental health had not improved significantly.

I was still in the same place I had been when I had taken a step back. My guilt and anxiety were at odds with each other, and fed each other. I knew the club was paying me a lot of money to play, not to sit on the sidelines, but I was stuck in the same dark hole, and the idea of returning to play only reintroduced the stress that had put me here in the first place. I was frustrated. *How can they not understand?*

Lisa told me that one of the great challenges with problems that people can't see is that they presume they aren't really there. It's much easier to empathise with someone who has a broken arm in a sling than with someone who says they have a sore back. To other people, I looked like my normal self, I talked like my normal self, I behaved like my normal self. But I didn't feel like myself at all. I missed more team training sessions at the club, in favour of conditioning sessions with the rehab coordinator, and I sensed the pressure mounting.

'But what's wrong now?' I was asked. 'Why can't you train with the group?'

I could only sigh, weary. 'The same thing that was wrong three weeks ago,' I replied. 'I haven't slept at all, in weeks.'

The shame of disappointing everyone was a big part of the reason I hadn't done anything about my issues for so long, and it was still strong, even now. But I knew that I couldn't train or play yet because I was barely capable of completing a simple running session—fatigue and my broken concentration levels left me feeling utterly useless.

It frustrated me enormously. The issues I was having were so fundamental, impacting the way I lived my life in every single moment, but to others they were invisible. I could see my coaches wrestling with it, limited by their own perspectives and trying to support me, but really wanting me to get better quickly so I could go back out on the field.

Ultimately, I decided to return to play. There was nothing else I could really do. *Just get through to the off-season and then you can get away*, I told myself. At least it would take the questions about returning off my plate.

On my return, nothing changed—not that I expected it to. My opening game was with the VFL side, against Essendon at Windy Hill. I played relatively well, kicking three goals in a narrow loss.

At quarter time, VFL coach Steve Grace came up to me with a great grin on his face. I had taken a big mark and goaled in the opening minutes. 'That must have felt good!' he said.

'Yeah,' I responded, but it hadn't really. I didn't feel anything, I was just out there doing my job.

As the season progressed, the VFL side qualified to play finals, the first of which was against Essendon at Port Melbourne. I kicked four goals in a tight victory. Anna congratulated me on the ride home. 'Well done, you played so well!' she said.

I told her I wished I hadn't. The thing that had stuck out to me most was the abuse I'd received all day from over the fence. I didn't have the emotional resilience to deal with the competitiveness and nastiness of football supporters, which rained down on me even though I had played well. It was like they smelled blood.

I felt guilty for saying it out loud, but I wanted it all to be over. All I wanted was to get away from the football world for a while—to head overseas, anywhere they didn't know me. It was my job to play well and I cared about my team-mates, who wanted to win, but there was no satisfaction in it for me.

The following week, we lost. By the next Tuesday morning I was on a plane, determined to leave every part of that season behind me.

11

TIME AND SPACE

Before I knew it, I was on holiday in America with Anna. The stresses and anxieties of the 2017 season drained away almost instantly—the weight of football couldn't follow me halfway across the world.

Anna and I were more connected than we had ever been before. I appreciated deeply how she had stuck by me through the worst moments of my life. It took someone special to be able to cope with everything the way she had, and I was beyond grateful. We had fun together, enjoying the change of scene and sharing new experiences. It was the first time I had felt like myself in a while.

We spent time in Los Angeles, then Las Vegas and New York. Owinda met us in New York, at the tail end of his own six-month-long holiday with nothing but a backpack and one pair of shoes. His holiday funds were running low, so he crashed on our couch in Soho, which gave us a good chance to catch up.

Owi had been away from Melbourne during much of my difficult period, and I had really missed him. We had communicated intermittently from the opposite sides of the globe, but it had been difficult to share with him what I was going through. I was relieved that he didn't treat me any differently now that everything was out in the open.

We spent many light-hearted nights at Bob & Ken's bar, around the corner from our hotel, trying to recreate scenes from our favourite sitcom, *How I Met Your Mother*. But one night we talked about what had happened to me while he was away, and why I had taken time off.

Like many people, Owi assumed that I had just cracked under the pressure of my contract and the weight of expectation that had come with it. That was part of it, but it wasn't the whole story. I told him how bad things had been for me—how the insomnia that had started years earlier had spiralled out of control, how my anxiety had resulted in panic attacks, how joyless every part of my life had become. I explained that my depression and anxiety seemed to be made much worse by football, but they hadn't been created by football. They were a much bigger issue. And I hadn't just had a couple of weeks off for a mid-season break—it had been a very dark year.

Owi was genuinely taken aback. He hadn't realised the severity of what I had been through.

As our trip came to an end and Anna and I headed home, that conversation stayed with me. *People don't really understand what happened*, I realised. It was easy to bundle up what I had been through into a tidy package—big contract, big pressure—because the only insight they had was that heavily scripted statement from the Bulldogs.

I realised that if I expected others to really understand, I needed to share more. It didn't have to be every excruciating detail, and I knew I wasn't obligated to say anything, but I felt it was worthwhile trying to explain how someone who looked like they had it so good could be feeling so bad.

When I returned to Australia, I met with James and Liam to discuss it. 'I want a way to share my story on my terms,' I told them. 'Because I feel like I left everyone without any explanation last year.'

They were hesitant; it was a risk to reopen the wound when everyone had likely moved on, they said.

I disagreed. 'Every single interview I do from now on, they're going to ask me about this,' I said. 'Everything that I do on the field is going to be painted with this brush. It's much better for me to go out there and be open about it than to leave people guessing about what actually happened.'

They took a little convincing, but eventually they came around to the idea. The question was how I was going to make this big statement. We talked about me going on

The Footy Show or another similar TV program, knowing that there would be a fee offered for an exclusive, but I wasn't interested in money; it was about sharing my story in a full and meaningful way.

In the end, we decided to do it via Gary Ablett Junior's new company, Exclusive Insight, a content platform that was set up to connect elite sportspeople directly with their audience. And so, late in 2017, before the next preseason had begun, I sat down for a filmed 45-minute interview, giving honest answers to questions about my mental health journey.

At the end of the session, I felt relief. I was surprised by how comfortable I'd felt as the words flowed out of me, how simple it was to answer questions about my most vulnerable experiences. It was honestly liberating. I had, for the first time, been able to choose the media, as opposed to the media choosing me. I wasn't wedged in between commercial breaks, or going where some journalist led me; I had the time and space to tell people exactly what I'd been through.

When it went out, the response was stunning. Hundreds if not thousands of people reacted to my story, on social media platforms and other channels, and while there was some negativity, I was overwhelmed by the volume of support. Sharing my story had helped me to process it, to answer the question I still had: 'Why did this happen?'

Without meaning to, I had also started a conversation for a lot of people who had been struggling themselves, or who knew someone who was struggling. 'My brother has been through this. My friend has. I have,' one person wrote. I was awed and proud, but as the messages poured in, I realised something terrifying: *I have no idea what to say to these people.*

I was inundated with requests from media organisations, and I started getting requests to be involved in mental health campaigns and awareness efforts. I had stumbled into a completely new world, one that I hadn't known existed only months earlier. It wasn't quite what I had intended when I sat down to talk about my struggles.

I did a campaign for Headspace and a candid interview with Bob Murphy on the Bulldogs' podcast, but after that I began to pull back from speaking publicly. I had said my piece. Now I had to focus on fitting back into a football club and preparing for the season ahead.

•

My customary fear of preseason had a different feel to it in late 2017. I still felt anxious about being fit enough and running a good time in our trial, but I also felt I had something to prove about my character. I needed to show the coaches that they could rely on me once more—that I wasn't on the verge of having a mental breakdown at any moment.

After an off-season spent working on how I felt about myself, I couldn't fathom the idea of sliding back to where I had been. I was determined to make the most of the work I had done, the sense of peace I'd managed to find. I felt a deep sense of responsibility to deliver for the club. I had taken my time away, I had got stronger, and I felt now I had to do the job that I'd been working towards since I was five years old.

•

I'd made a plan with Lisa to give myself the best chance of coping with the challenges I faced as an athlete, now and into the future. What Lisa and I discussed was trying to recreate the balance and productivity that I had when I was finishing high school, which I realised was the last time in my life when I'd felt consistently happy.

When I was a kid, I'd told her, I always played my worst basketball during the school holidays, when I didn't have anything else to focus on. Dad always said he'd played better football when he'd worked the morning before a game. I needed all the parts of my brain to be firing to be at my best, so one aspect of my plan for 2018 was to go back to university.

The year before, I had started a business management course at Victoria University, and as tedious as it could be at times, it gave me a sense of purpose outside of football. Walking into those classrooms made me feel normal. People recognised me occasionally, but for the most part I was just another student trying to finish his assignments on time and get decent grades. With time, my confidence grew and I started answering questions and interacting with other students. Eventually it almost felt like I was back at school again.

At the club, I found preseason to be as hard as ever, but it yielded results. I began to feel stronger and more capable as the grinding training schedule rolled on through the summer heat. Slowly but surely, I built my fitness base and found my confidence to play again, but I was resigned to having to come through the reserves to begin the season.

I showed consistent improvement, and the months of training were relatively uneventful, barring a soft-tissue injury to my glute and the ongoing issues with my lower back. In previous years, it could spasm so severely that I would miss a week of training, but it wasn't constant. This year seemed different. When it spasmed, the pain was sharp and would diminish considerably with some medication and rest, but it never went away completely. I worked closely with the physios to address the problem, but nothing seemed to help. It was a growing background noise.

Starting the season in the reserves was a challenging prospect. No one was saying it out loud, but I knew I needed to prove myself.

And I made an unflattering beginning, struggling to make the most of my early VFL practice games. I felt out of touch, but I found form in Round 2, in a game against Coburg at Whitten Oval in epically bad weather. It was warm and the wind was blowing 50 knots from the south—we kicked into it in the first quarter and managed to draw even. At quarter time, the coach told us to adjust our ball movement for the wind: 'Don't bomb it long!'

As he spoke, the wind swung around 180 degrees and the rain began to pour down on our heads. It wasn't until the end of the coach's eight-minute address that he realised the wind had changed.

'Never mind, boys, same as the first quarter!' he barked.

I was placed in the middle of the ground as a midfielder and attended a few centre bounces. I thrived in my newfound freedom, dividing my time between rucking, playing forward and playing in the midfield, finishing the day with over twenty disposals and five goals. It was the first time in forever that I had genuinely thought, *Fuck it, I'm just going to have fun*—and it had worked.

It was the happiest I'd felt after a game of football in a long time.

•

I presumed I would be playing in the VFL again the following week, but Bevo pulled me aside and said this week's Round 5 match against Fremantle was a good one for me to return to the AFL side. 'I think it makes sense, playing over in Perth. It feels right to bring you back this week,' he said.

I was bewildered. *What does the location have to do with it?*

I thought. *AFL football is just as hard in every state, in my experience.* But I didn't care—I hadn't played for the AFL side since I had taken time off, 290 days earlier.

I spent much of the lead-up to the game thinking about how people would react, how the crowd would treat me. I had seen the best and worst of a fired-up West Australian crowd—they were as passionate as any crowd I'd ever played in front of (Adelaide came a close second)—but I had never played at their brand new, state-of-the-art stadium.

Unlike at Subiaco, the former home ground for Fremantle and West Coast, the stands at Optus Stadium were completely vertical so that the fans towered over you. In games gone by in Perth, I had felt immersed in the crowd, unable to escape their vitriol. I could hear every word that was said to me, and going to the players' bench felt like walking directly into the crowd as they abused me. Optus Stadium didn't feel like that at all, and I was relieved. It was depersonalised, in a way. The separation between the crowd and the players was healthier.

Unfortunately, the match was a shocking one for us. We kicked just eight goals for the day, lost by 54 points and had half as many shots on goal as Freo—a complete and utter disaster. I had played okay, managing to kick two of our goals, but I'd also missed a couple that would have made me prouder of my individual performance. I spent most of the day marked by my former Premiership teammate Joel Hamling, who was now playing for Fremantle, but with the lead blowing out early in the game, the pressure was off and we fell into some gentle ribbing, back and forth.

I had missed Joel. We had come to the Bulldogs at the same time—him from Geelong and me from the Giants. He had never taken life too seriously. He was from Broome originally, and still had that knockabout, easygoing nature. In retrospect, I realised that Joel had the approach to football that I wished I'd had: work when you need to but don't get bogged down in the details. Keep things in perspective.

After such a bad team performance, I didn't feel too much pressure around my spot for the next game. I hadn't set the world on fire—seven disposals for two goals was hardly something to write home about—but there were many others who would be under more scrutiny. I had taken a solid enough step, and I would solidify my spot in the side in the coming weeks, but not as a forward. I shifted into the ruck, playing solo in most games.

As the season wore on, the workload took a significant toll on my body. Every game was a battle, and my back was deteriorating rapidly with the smashing and crashing of each centre bounce and ruck contest. My recovery after games was getting harder each week: first I was stiff, then I was sore, then I found I could barely get out of bed the day after a game. I managed it as best as I could with the medical staff.

We tried simple things at first, like anti-inflammatory medication and icing, but they no longer seemed to be making a difference. Epidurals were enormously effective initially, but their effect soon wore off and then they too stopped working. We decreased my training load early in the week to focus on reactivating my core muscles, avoiding any exercises or movements that would bring on acute pain, and the physios taped my back most days to stop my disc pain from flaring up, but that meant I was unable to bend over.

Even with the support I had, things continued to deteriorate. My game-day performances were more and more compromised. I would start having spasms down my left leg in the middle of a game, then would struggle to change direction or jump.

It was yet another injury that was hard to see—I couldn't point to a scan and say, 'There, you see? That's where I'm hurt.' As hard as they tried, the medical team couldn't fix it, and I became frustrated. The best they could do was to put a band-aid on the problem, and it simply wasn't getting better. At the same time, I was losing fitness. I was barely training during the week, and simply playing games wasn't enough to keep me in peak condition.

Sure enough, in Round 11, I felt my calf grab at the end of the first quarter. I was almost certain I had torn it. It was my left calf, the same side that had suffered ankle injuries since I was eighteen. I played through the game, although on limited minutes, helping my team to a miserable 49-point loss.

I felt horrible—there's nothing worse than getting injured early in a game and feeling like a genuine liability. But what made this feeling worse was my knowledge that the injury had been virtually inevitable. It was bound to happen, given my dismal program for the previous couple of months.

•

The following day, I went down to Victoria House Medical Imaging to get a scan on my calf. A call from Gary Zimmerman later didn't go as expected.

'Tommy, the scan looks pretty good,' he said. 'A bit of a bleed, but not in the area of concern you were describing. You should be good to go this week.'

I was happy to hear I could play but confused about my injury. 'Why is it so sore, Gaz?' I asked. 'I can barely walk today—there has to be something wrong with it!'

I panicked at the thought that he might think my injury wasn't real. I couldn't bear the thought that my teammates or coaches might think I had checked out on them for no reason. *Have I imagined it?* I wondered for a brief second. I leaned down to feel my calf, and sure enough, it was painful to touch. It felt like it was in a permanent cramp and I was hobbling as I walked.

'Tommy, it's okay,' Gary said. 'It's probably a neural issue, coming from your back. It's referring tightness all the way down your left side and causing this issue. We'll get on top of it this week.'

Gary had always been so good at supporting players,

and I felt calmer knowing he was on my side. Unfortunately, I didn't realise what 'getting on top of it' meant. Chris Bell obliterated my calf that week, trying to reduce the tightness. We had a session most days, and I experienced some of the more excruciating pain I had been put through on a physio's table. By the end of the sessions, I was sweating from pain, and him from the physical exertion.

But, sure enough, the pain began to clear up, and by the end of the week I was able to train again. With a bye that weekend, I was confident of returning to play against Port Adelaide in the following round.

•

I packed my bag for Adelaide feeling much better. My calf had settled dramatically and I was ready to play.

We had struggled all season, with just four wins and seven losses. Winning seemed a more daunting task with every round that passed, and once again the game did not go well. A late-game ruck contest against Patty Ryder only worsened the experience for me—I compound-dislocated my finger. Blood spurted everywhere and an intense pain shot through my hand.

Having experienced a compound-dislocation before, I knew what to do. I pulled hard on my finger, popped it back into place, and walked from the ground with my hand over my head, blood flowing. Game over. I flew home early with Lucas Webb so I could get surgery the following day.

I figured I would miss the following round, but after surgery the club created a hard-shelled plastic brace to protect my finger. A painkilling injection numbed it for training, so I could test out how it felt. I was cleared to play against North Melbourne the following week, as we looked to break what was now a four-game losing streak.

We lost against the Kangaroos but won against Geelong the following week, only to fall back onto the losers' list against Hawthorn in Round 16. My finger was braced and my back continued to spiral, the pain now an everyday fact of my existence. I couldn't bend and I couldn't play. I missed the following week against Melbourne as a result, and at that point the scrutiny began to rise.

Prominent football journalist Damian Barrett was one of the first to comment, on social media:

> IF back soreness is the real reason Boyd is not playing this weekend . . . THEN that's a shame. Would've liked to have seen him up against [Max] Gawn. Instead, [Jordan] Roughead, who Bevo has developed a set against, will go up against a guy who may be the best ruckman in the game.

If? I was so tired of the merry-go-round. I didn't care what Damian wrote—he was a journalist, and it was his job to create headlines. I had been dealing with my back injury for years and it had never been worse, I knew that. Bevo defended me, trying to protect one of his highest-profile players, as everyone expected him to. Verbal shots were fired, but everyone was just doing their job. Meanwhile, all I could think was: *This is the exact reason why I don't enjoy playing football anymore.*

It was a feeling I had stubbornly denied for a long time, but I couldn't ignore it anymore. I hated the attention. I hated the politics and the scrutiny. I didn't expect special treatment from the media, I just wanted to get away from it. The fact that two senior members of the AFL industry were squabbling over me with such passion seemed ridiculous, especially as I didn't feel the same passion for the game.

•

My final game of the year came the following week, in Round 18 against West Coast. I barely made it through, and it was leagues away from my best performances.

Chris Bell sat me down in the aftermath and said, 'Tommy, we are going to need to do something about this back. We can't keep going round and round in circles as we have been.'

I agreed. I couldn't keep playing in so much pain, as it was impacting my life outside of football: the chronic pain and frustration were weighing heavily on my mental and emotional state. Something had to give.

We agreed that I would step back from playing until my back issues were under control, and so we set about making a holistic plan to get me there. I would no longer train with my team, no longer play at AFL level, but would focus instead on an intensive program of Pilates, swimming and specialised weights and cross-training.

I wasn't planning to sit out the rest of the season, but once I stopped playing it was like I lost momentum and all the issues with my back just became more obvious. The remaining rounds crawled by listlessly. I was struggling, and so was the team—we lost eight players to injury and finished thirteenth on the ladder, with eight wins and fourteen losses. Our Premiership felt like a distant memory.

I went into the off-season with some pain, but the lack of jumping and football work during my break had helped me—without the heavy load through my lower back, things seemed to improve. I did my best not to think about football at all, but as another preseason approached and my training schedule increased, the same problems arose all over again.

I returned to the club ahead of our official start date to work through it with the physio, but I felt a great wave of dread building inside of me. For once I wasn't worried about training or trials or measurements. I just couldn't bear the thought of another twelve months dealing with the same back issues.

Sure enough, when preseason started, it was Groundhog Day for me. My schedule was much the same as it had been as the 2018 season ended: swimming, Pilates, strength, cross-training. I began a running program but was so limited in sprinting, jumping, twisting and turning that I really couldn't do any proper football training. I was almost completely isolated from my team as a result.

I could sense the coaches' frustration. They needed me back in the game—and anyway, *he should have been fixed by now, right?* Every week that passed, every step closer to the AFL season, their pressure and frustration only mounted, yet every day I left the club with as much pain as when I had arrived, if not more.

The medical staff pulled out all the stops. They wanted to help me, as they sensed my deep frustration and they too were under pressure from the club, but there was such marginal progress that it was hard to remain optimistic. I did what I was told, following my program, but almost daily now I had the thought, *Why are you doing this?* It was a nagging voice in the back of my head, and as I looked at the difficult road ahead it was only getting louder.

One day, as I watched another training session from the sidelines with Gary Zimmerman, I decided to raise it with him. 'I don't want to do this anymore, mate. I'm always in pain, and I really am not enjoying this.'

Gary considered this for a moment and gave me some advice. 'Tommy, listen, you shouldn't make a decision like that when you're in rehab,' he advised. 'It wasn't that long ago that you were out there playing good footy. Get back to playing, then if you still feel this way, you'll know it's the right decision.'

The only other person I had spoken to about this was Anna, and she didn't have an opinion either way. I could see the wisdom in what Gary had told me, so I decided to give it one more go. I needed to get back on the field once more, to see if there was anything still there for me.

I redoubled my efforts, I worked, but the grind of rehabilitation didn't get any easier. I spent most nights in agony. I could only sleep on my back, to alleviate the stress on my lower back. I couldn't do anything easily at home. At the club, I was a shadow of my best self. It felt like I was at about 50 per cent capacity on a good day; on a bad day I could barely run. The days had little to no joy in them, and the monotony of work wore me down as much as the pain and frustration.

I couldn't see anything good ahead of me, and I couldn't see any scenario where I would play decent AFL football again. Without that faith, I lost focus. My diet slipped and I gained weight. Any memory of my love for football had long faded away, yet I carried on, I held on. I approached my return through the VFL with some trepidation, but it was inevitable. I just had to get out there and see how I felt.

•

My first game back, against Collingwood's VFL side in April 2019, was a disaster. I was slow, I couldn't bend, I couldn't run.

I had lost my greatest advantage as a player, which was my ability to jump. It was horrible, but I kept going.

I played against Williamstown two weeks later, a windy affair at their home ground. There were over 100 stoppages for the day as the wind pinned the ball to the grandstand side of the ground. It was my first full game since July 2018 and I was absolutely dominated by Williamstown's ruckman. I was exhausted. I was easily outclassed and felt pathetic.

I wasn't close to playing good VFL football, let alone AFL, and I didn't see that changing quickly. It wasn't just my lack of fitness, or my lack of mobility. I had lost the will to play. I no longer had a reason to get out there and struggle through four quarters of football.

My review wasn't good after the Williamstown game, and rightfully so. But the most stinging criticism came at the Bulldogs' Thursday morning training session, as the entire squad warmed up on the craft floor. Bevo approached me. We hadn't spoken in quite some time.

'What happened on Saturday, mate?' he asked.

I shrugged. 'What do you mean?'

'You looked tired—he completely outclassed you,' Bevo told me straight.

'I was tired,' I said defensively. 'There were over a hundred stoppages, and that was my first full game back.'

I was tense. This wasn't a conversation I was expecting as I warmed up to train, and I felt ambushed in front of the rest of the team. We could have had this conversation all week—there had been ample opportunities. *Why is he doing this now?*

'Mate, he's a VFL ruckman,' Bevo persisted. 'He only does this part-time. You've beaten him in the past—I don't understand it.' He was clearly frustrated. The situation was escalating quickly, and many eyes were on us as it played out.

'Listen, mate, I don't know what you want to hear from me,' I said hotly. 'I haven't played in six months and I've barely been able to train. I played against a ruckman who has dominated the VFL for ten years on a day where there were repeat stoppages all game. What do you want me to say?'

Neither of us was going to back down, so we dropped the conversation, fiercely annoyed, and went out to train.

I was livid for the rest of the day. Many of my teammates came up to offer me support, but it didn't help. It wasn't just the interaction with Bevo or the timing of it that was eating away at me. The problem was that he had every right to be frustrated. I wasn't up to standard. I wasn't fit enough. It wasn't all my fault, but for sure some of it was. I had lost interest, so how could I strive for excellence? I was no longer simply frustrated by parts of my job—I loathed them. I just didn't care to deal with the worst of it anymore. And I knew that there was no room for passengers in a club that was trying to succeed, especially not one taking up as much of their salary cap as I was.

•

The horrible mix of emotions that I felt served as a great distraction from the game I was playing in two days' time. I felt some level of self-respect because I had stood up for myself. I hadn't let myself be trampled. But the more I thought about it, the more convinced I was that we could have had that conversation at a different time, without an audience.

I also felt guilt and shame. As much as I wanted to believe that Bevo was the issue, that Bevo was wrong, I couldn't. I was the problem. Specifically, my lack of desire to play AFL football and my years of back issues were the problem. I was all but certain that the VFL game at the MCG on the weekend would be my last.

I searched for any scrap of meaning, joy or purpose during that game—some tiny indication that my future still lay in the AFL—but I didn't find any. Nothing had changed since the week before. I was flat, unfit, unable to jump and hampered by the same pain in my back that had been tormenting me for months. The only bright light in another disappointing game was a beautiful set shot goal I kicked from outside 50—but even as it landed, it felt like a distant memory.

I was teetering on the brink, but I just needed a final push. I got it the following Tuesday afternoon. Before our training session, Chris Maple and Chris Grant, two senior managers in the football department, pulled me aside and told me they wanted to meet with me afterwards. I knew it wasn't going to be good. When I sat down with them later, Chris Maple got straight to it: 'Tom, you're not where you need to be, body-wise. We're seeing improvements, but not enough.'

'I know,' I said flatly. 'I haven't been watching my diet well enough.'

They seemed surprised at the admission.

'Well, at least you're honest,' Chris Grant said. 'Most players in this situation say they've been doing everything right.'

They weren't attacking me, they weren't yelling, we were just having a conversation. I could sense that they wanted to work with me, not against me, and I appreciated that. They were doing their job, and I hadn't been—I could admit that much.

They laid out their plan for me, a six-week 'mini pre-season' to get me back to match fitness. They would give me all the support that I needed to get fit again. Chris Grant said, 'Look, Tom, you're only young, but it's starting to look like—'

'Like my career's a flash in the pan?' I interrupted.

They both sat back in shock. 'No,' Chris continued, 'I was going to say that it's starting to look like this year is going to be a waste, and we can't have that from one of our most important players. We need you out there, mate.'

I nodded. 'It would have been a fair comment, though.'

I appreciated the care and consideration that they had put into the discussion, their plan and my football future.

But I knew instantly there was no way in hell that I was going to do it. My mind flashed to the future—the media scrutiny, my teammates' disappointment in me. *Nope*, I thought. *This is no longer my path.*

•

I left the club without talking to anyone else. I had a uni class half an hour later, so I drove to the campus and parked in the car park. There was no one around. Beside me, four lanes of traffic whizzed past on Ballarat Road.

As I watched it, I considered what I was about to do. I was almost certain of my decision, but it was still hard to make. *Am I really doing this? Is this how my AFL career is going to end?* I tried a final moment of soul searching, looking for any semblance of doubt. When I found none, I picked up the phone and called Lisa Stevens, and explained what had happened over the past week.

She empathised with how I felt, but before we got too deep in conversation, I told her, 'It's okay—I'm going to retire.'

I had wondered when I made the call if Lisa might try to change my mind or tell me to reconsider, but she didn't. It was my decision, she said, and she added that with everything I had gone through in the last two or three years, it was hardly a surprising one. 'Would you like me to help you?' she asked.

I thought about it. In times past, I had let other people make the calls for me, but it felt like I needed to do this on my own—to do it properly and do it right. I politely declined. Next I called Anna to tell her what I was going to do, and then I walked into my business class. I felt more excited about walking into that classroom than I'd felt about football for months.

After the class, I called Dad. It was the hardest of all the calls I had to make, because I knew he wouldn't understand. 'Dad, I'm going retire,' I told him. 'I don't want to do this anymore, and there's no way that I'm going to continue.'

He was silent for a second. 'Really?' he said.

'Yes, mate. It's the decision I've made. I'm just trying to work out what to do next.'

In previous years, I would have asked Dad for permission or advice. But this time I wasn't asking him, I was telling him, and I didn't leave much room for discussion.

'Have you really thought about this?' he asked me.

'You know I've been thinking about this for years,' I replied. 'So yes, I'm sure.'

We talked about the next steps. I wanted to bite the bullet and call Peter Gordon, but Dad said that could wait—that I should call my manager Liam first and let him talk to Peter, then I could meet with them both together to work through it.

I agreed, and rang Liam. He understood, and didn't put up much of a fight. He promised to call Peter straight afterwards.

Later, Liam told me that before he'd had the chance to say anything, Peter said, 'Tom's going to retire, isn't he?'

The next day I found myself back at Peter's house with my father and Liam—in the same place, with the same people, as when I'd started my Bulldogs career. Once again, I found myself going through the details of a contract, though this time it was about the termination of one, not the conception. The mood was heavy. There was a lot of history between us all, good and bad, but we had shared the ultimate football success together, and that would bind us forever.

The meeting didn't take too long. Peter agreed to facilitate things from the club's end. There was a small amount of back and forth around the wording of the official statements, but beyond that it was a simple agreement: the club would release me from my contract, and I would release the club from the obligation of paying it.

As soon as the formalities were over, the mood changed entirely and all the tension evaporated. I greatly admired Peter and considered him a friend and mentor. It felt right to me that it was him seeing it through to the end.

•

Up to that point, it still hadn't really dawned on me what my decision meant, but now I felt the weight of it. Besides the money I was handing back, the moment marked the end of my career as a footballer, a career I had worked towards and worked on for as long as I could remember. Every decision I had made to that day had been, in some way, shape or form, about playing AFL football. This one wasn't. Before any doubt or regret could set in, I thought about what my future would have looked like if I'd continued trying to recover the passion and capability to perform that I had lost, and I knew I was doing the right thing.

I thought about players who'd had long-lasting careers in the AFL. The ones I had met all had a deep and unwavering passion for the game. They were either obsessive or genuinely in love with their profession. If I was honest with myself, I had never really felt that during my time in the AFL. There were very few games in my professional career in which I felt the joyful lightness that football had given me as a junior player. The 2016 Grand Final was one, and that VFL game against Coburg in 2018 was another, but it was hard to think of many more. Whatever magic ingredient went into those games was not obvious to me, nor could I recreate it.

The thought of remaining an AFL player while I knew and accepted all of this was intolerable. I couldn't stay and continue to disappoint my teammates, my coaches and the club. I couldn't hold on in the hope of a miracle change of perspective. It was over.

•

The next day, the Western Bulldogs released the following statement on my behalf:

> My decision to retire now is a reflection of issues I've had over the past five years both with physical injury and with mental health, and they have now accumulated to a point where I just don't have the desire to play or the enjoyment of the game I used to have.
>
> I've spoken with key people at the Western Bulldogs and my close friends and family, and I am satisfied that this is the right decision for my future. I approached the Club about my desire to retire and be released from my contract this week, and we have worked out a mutually agreeable position.
>
> I'm grateful to both the Giants and the Bulldogs for allowing me the opportunity to experience playing football at the highest level. I have received unbelievable support from the players, coaches and staff at the Western Bulldogs, particularly over the last couple of years, which I will always appreciate.
>
> Leaving the game as a Premiership player is something I will always be proud of, along with all the enduring relationships I have forged and the memories I have created along the way.

I didn't think too much of the statement. The most important conversations I'd had were with the people I was closest to at the football club—the media coverage didn't mean that much to me. I knew the public commentary would focus on the one mention of mental health in my statement, even though that had not really been a factor in my decision, but that was the easy angle. I understood. What was ironic was that I felt stronger mentally and more in control than I had in years.

I had so much that I wanted to do in my life, and football had prevented me from starting that journey. Playing the game is worth it if you love it, but I now accepted that it wasn't for me. It made no sense to linger, for any amount of money.

•

In my time in the AFL, I had seen some of the game's heroes playing their final matches—guys like Matthew Boyd and Bob Murphy. Their retirement speeches were heartfelt and filled with emotion. They had given their entire careers and every ounce of themselves to their club and to the game, and you felt it when they left. I couldn't even pretend to compare myself with guys like that.

When thinking through what I wanted to say to the group at the Bulldogs, I knew that it had to be honest and address the reality of the situation—that my career had not been a success. It had been a struggle from day one, and I'd had the incredible good fortune of achieving Premiership glory along the way. With that in mind, I felt comfortable walking into the football club one last time and standing in front of my teammates to say goodbye.

'I've been lucky enough to be a part of a Premiership team, and that's something that I will always be proud of,' I told them. 'But I really . . . I just wanted to say that I hope all of you know that you're not the reason I am leaving. If anything, you're all part of the reason I lasted this long. So thank you.'

The room felt heavy, and I didn't want to leave it that way. This wasn't a sad moment—it was the beginning of a new chapter for me and for the club.

'By the way,' I said, 'if any of you are thinking of negotiating a new contract, now would be a good time!'

I was glad I could make them laugh. The final moments of my AFL career ended with a smile, which was all I could have asked for.

When I left Whitten Oval that day, I was no longer a professional footballer, but I had Anna by my side and my whole life ahead of me. Football had given me so much, but my time in the game was over. I was excited for what was to come. I had the smallest amount of nerves, for sure, but not a single grain of doubt.

EPILOGUE

My AFL football career was a disappointment. It was disappointing for the clubs that paid my salary, for the fans who desperately wanted me to win, and for the media who built me up from a young age to be a star of the game. But more than anything, my football career was disappointing to me, because I had believed it would make me happy, and it didn't.

Still, as challenging as it was, my time in football taught me more than anything else in my life ever has. It taught me about myself and what I value, and about others and how I interact with them. As I look back now, I see that my career forced me to grow.

When I was young and aspiring to become a professional athlete, I never had enough time to sit back and understand who I was, what I wanted to do and how I was going to do it. Every accomplishment, every step along the way only lent itself to one thing: whatever came next. It was intoxicating to ride the roller-coaster of life, to jump from one thing to another, always moving forward, always aiming for the next goal, achieving it and aiming higher.

But living that way didn't lend itself to any self-reflection, at least not for me. As I strove to accomplish everything I had ever wanted, as quickly as possible, I forgot to accomplish the thing that would serve me best in years to come, which was understanding who I was as a person. From the age of five, I had dreamed of just one thing—to play in the AFL—so there was nothing more terrifying than the first time I realised, after eighteen years of dreaming, that I didn't want to play in the AFL after all.

I retired from professional football on 16 May 2019. I was 23 years old, being paid $1 million a year, with two and a half seasons remaining on my contract. Many people told me I was insane. Although I knew I had made the right decision, I was left with the question: *If I'm not an AFL footballer, what am I?*

By the time I retired, I knew that I was more than that label—that's what football taught me. I realised that I had other passions in my life that, until that point, I had been unable to explore. I had discovered that I loved working with people, watching them grow and improve, but also being able to grow and improve myself.

I wanted my life to be about more than just kicks, marks and goals, even if some of the most exciting and happy moments of my life had happened on a football field. I was determined to do something different with my life, rather than hanging on and hoping that I could just 'make it work'. I wanted to thrive, not survive, in the profession I chose—and regardless of what anyone else was telling me, even if they all thought I was crazy, I was determined to make the next chapter of my life the best one yet.

•

Not long after I retired, I was invited to speak to a group of schoolkids about football, mental health, and the highs and lows of being a professional athlete. I agreed to do it because it was important to me to tell my story and talk about the struggles I went through, and the happiness I felt when I decided to depart the AFL.

I knew when I left football that I wanted to help people, that I wanted to continue sharing my emotional and mental challenges in the hope that doing so might help others—and young people in particular. After all, if a six-foot-seven, 21-year-old, million-dollar-a-year, Premiership hero, number 1 draft pick, AFL footballer, from a loving family, with a beautiful and supportive life partner (and so on) could have the challenges I did, then anyone could, right?

Difficult as the speechwriting process was, I found it therapeutic. As I finished writing about each part of my life and career, it felt like I was closing one door and opening another. Putting my story together, I felt challenged in a new and positive way. *What do people need to know? What parts of the story are going to be valuable to others? What is valuable to me?*

Then came the process of trying to work through how I actually *felt* during those times, and figuring out how to articulate those things.

Finally, I came to the really hard part: what was the point of all this? What was I trying to say? I asked myself: *Am I trying to tell people how to live their lives?* No.

Am I trying to tell everyone how hard my life has been? No, definitely not.

What about what I have learned? Kind of . . .

And what have I learned? Well, in the simplest terms, that it's okay to not be okay.

My career had been full of doubt and uncertainty, but I had survived it. I had grown. I learned that overcoming something was only half the battle: the rest lies in understanding *why* something happened, and what to do differently next time.

I learned about the power of taking stock every once in a while, of sifting through the mess of your past, keeping what you need and throwing out the rest, so you can move forward stronger and better able to tackle today, and the tomorrows after that.

•

In March 2020, when the pandemic hit, life shifted again. My speaking engagements were the first things to be cancelled or postponed, then local sport, then my study. I postponed a renovation, and later my and Anna's wedding (we postponed it twice, in the end). Soon, like everyone else, I put my life completely on hold. I would be lying if I said I didn't feel lost during this time, or that I wasn't scared and concerned about the future.

After some time sifting through the various emotions that the global pandemic brought out of me, I realised I still had something that I wanted to say—that there were un-resolved issues I hadn't dealt with, lessons I had half-learned but never expressed. The book you have just read was born in those moments of uncertainty.

When I decided to write it, I wanted to poke as many holes as I could in the 'number 1 draft pick, million-dollar player' image that everyone knew. I wanted to describe the experience from the inside, so that people could see my humanity. So this hasn't been a story about how unique my life was, but rather how I am just like everyone else—subject to stress and struggle, disappointment and failure, as well as happiness, friendship, love and all the wonderful things that life has to offer.

So I began to write about my experiences—all the thoughts I wished I had never had, the feelings I wished I could have suppressed. It was uncomfortable, at times difficult, and more than once, locked in the bedroom I had converted into an office, I put my head in my hands and wondered if it was all worth it. Almost two years later, with the help of a wonderful editor, I am proud to say I finished this book.

Later, reflecting on the journey that led me to understand what I had been thinking and feeling over all those years, I realised that it had not been an easy process, but it was certainly a worthwhile one. It makes me think about how difficult a task we have as people to be kind to ourselves and one another, to understand each other. Staying aware of the humanity of other people is a lesson I relearn every day. You can never truly know what someone is going through, nor what they are thinking or feeling at any moment in time—not their grief, their trauma, their triumphs or their joy. But I think it's important to try—to put yourself in their shoes and remember that everyone is going through something.

I hope this book gives you a window into what I was thinking and how I was feeling when the world was telling me my life was perfect. My life wasn't how it looked, and no one's really is, because the image rarely matches the reality of someone's lived experience.

Along the way, some things worked out the way I planned them, but mostly they didn't. The dreams I had never really matched the reality of the life that I have lived so far, but that's okay. We all have to deal with reality. And reality is fine with me.

Lifeline is a national charity providing all Australians experiencing emotional distress with access to crisis support and suicide prevention services. We are committed to empowering Australians to be suicide-safe through connection, compassion and hope. We are here to listen, without judgement and to advocate for equal opportunities for mental wellbeing. To learn more or to access support visit lifeline.org.au

Printed in Great Britain
by Amazon